The
Guide to

SPY
STUFF

The Pocket Guide to

SPY STUFF

Bart King

Illustrations by Russell Miller

GIBBS SMITH
TO ENRICH AND INSPIRE HUMANKIND

DEDICATION

This book is dedicated to
Lieutenant Colonel Gordon H. Bowen (USAF).

First Edition

22 21 20 19 18   5 4 3 2 1

Text © 2018 Bart King

Illustrations © 2018 Russell Miller

Published by
Gibbs Smith
P.O. Box 667
Layton, Utah 84041

1.800.835.4993 orders
www.gibbs-smith.com

Designed by Sky Hatter
Cover designed by Tom Deja

Gibbs Smith books are printed on either recycled, 100% post-consumer waste,
FSC-certified papers or on paper produced from sustainable PEFC-certified
forest/controlled wood source. Learn more at www.pefc.org.

Library of Congress Cataloging-in-Publication Data

Names: King, Bart, 1962- author. | Miller, Russell, illustrator.
Title: The pocket guide to spy stuff / Bart King ; illustrations by Russell Miller.
Description: First edition. | Layton, Utah : Gibbs Smith, [2018]
Identifiers: LCCN 2018001281 | ISBN 9781423649823 (pbk.)
Subjects: LCSH: Spies--Juvenile literature. | Espionage--Juvenile literature.
Classification: LCC JF1525.I6 K565 2018 | DDC 327.12--dc23
LC record available at https://lccn.loc.gov/2018001281

Contents

DANGER IS MY NICKNAME!

Hey, can you hold still for a second? This book is electronically scanning your right eye to figure out your security clearance. (You've heard of e-books, right?)

While it's doing that, let me ask you a question. Imagine a situation where you come to a door marked "Do Not Enter."

What do you do?

a. You enter cautiously.
b. You do not enter.
c. You ask a trusted pet if you should enter.

What do you say?[1]

While we wait for your security clearance, let me tell you about my spy credentials. First, I am an expert in *sabotage* (SAB-uh-taj), the art of destroying or damaging things for spy-ish reasons. My list of accomplishments includes derailing a toy train and blowing up a pumpkin.

Furthermore, I can kill with my bare feet (although I prefer not to step on caterpillars if I can help it). And while I can't confirm or deny any more details on my background, I *can* tell you that I'm a writer . . . and trust me, writers are spies!

The difference is that a writer wants to discover secrets and then share them with *everybody*. A spy usually wants to discover secrets and then share them with almost *nobody*.

Hey, it looks like this book's eye scan is done, and—uh-oh: you're not cleared for any top secret material at all! That's too bad. So please stop reading right now.

Did you hear what I said?

Well, I guess *that's* not going to work.

Wait! By continuing to read despite my warning, you've proven your interest in discovering hidden secrets. And

---

1. If you answered a or c, this is the book for you. (But if you answered b, you *really* need this book!)

SPIES: THE EXCEPTION TO THE RULE

Many people automatically dislike anyone who has the word "agent" in his or her job title. Press agent, talent agent, chemical agent . . . we hate 'em all! Do you know the only exception to this? Secret agents!

that's good enough for me! After all, learning secrets is why most spies get into spying. Because being one up on everyone else is pretty cool.

Of course, not all spies want to be cool. Some just don't have any choice! For example, a man named Bin Wu was once caught trying to smuggle night-vision equipment out of the United States and into China.

But here's what's amazing: Bin Wu *hated* the Chinese government! In fact, Bin Wu had been arrested in China for protesting China's policies. The Chinese gave Bin Wu a choice: either work as a secret agent for China, or go to prison for a long time. (Guess which one he picked?)

According to this book's electronic scan, you're an honest person. So maybe you don't think you're cut out for spying. Think again! If you've read this far, you're almost ready to trade in your Goody Two-Shoes for spy boots with poison gas canisters hidden in their heels. And then you'll be ready to do something *really* glamorous, like writing up a spy report.

Nobody knows what the first spy report was. But the oldest one we know of was written 4,000 years ago on a clay tablet somewhere in what is now Iraq. (It was a secret plan to watch for fire signals on the Euphrates River.)

My guess is that the *actual* oldest spy report was from hundreds of thousands of years ago and went something like this:

"Commander Thok, I am ready to give my report."

"Go ahead, Agent Boomp."

"I saw Reegu collecting shells!"

"Good work! Uh, why do you think Reegu was doing this?"

"Maybe he wants to start using the shells for money?"

"But that would totally destroy our current system of buying and selling items using very small rocks!"

"Perhaps Reegu just thinks seashells are pretty."

"They are, aren't they? I especially like the curly ones with the blue insides. *pause* But we should probably hit Reegu over the head with something hard just to be safe."

As we have learned from these early humans, spying is very exciting. It combines danger, secrecy, and the potential for making *really* big mistakes. And in modern times, spies get to wear cool sunglasses!

WHY SPY?

But cool sunglasses alone don't explain spying. The fact is that every nation wants to protect its borders and its citizens. Here are three ways nations can do this:

a. Make treaties with other countries.

b. Have a military.

c. Spy!

While I don't know for certain that cave people used spies, ancient civilizations did. For example, Greek mythology had the story of the demigod named Prometheus (pro-MEETH-ee-us). He stole secret technology (namely fire) from the head god, Zeus. Then Prometheus gave this classified information to the humans. Finally, after getting caught, Prometheus was sentenced to having his liver eaten by an eagle. Just like spies today!

And in between screams, I'll bet Prometheus would have agreed with the words of ancient Chinese leader Sun Tzu: "An army without secret agents is like a man without eyes and ears."

Hey, did you see that? "Eyes and ears." So *that's* why spies need sunglasses and earpieces.

Okay, now we understand why nations have spies. But I have to point out something before going onward. People like me love to learn about the secrets and failures of spies throughout history. But for every flub or mistake that a spy or spy agency makes, there are countless times when they save lives, foil enemy plots, and otherwise do exactly what people *hope* they will do.

So why don't we hear more about spies saving the day? To explain, you need to know about the most famous American spy group . . .

KNOW YOUR SPY AGENCIES!

There are 17 different US intelligence agencies. But when people think of American spies, they usually think of the **Central Intelligence Agency** (CIA). Its agents are in charge of spying outside of the United States.

The CIA's unofficial motto is: "Our failures are publicized. Our successes are not." See, good spies want to keep their successes *secret*. So don't think that all spies are dangerous, bumbling nincompoops, because only a few of them are. And the spies who are really good at their jobs are the ones you'll *never* hear about. (Like me!)

BTW, one of the busiest Starbucks in the nation is inside the CIA headquarters. Usually at a Starbucks, the barista will ask for your name. But not at CIA Starbucks. (Secret agents don't like to give their names!) The best-selling drink at CIA Starbucks is a vanilla latte. So if you ever go there, say "I want my latte shaken, not stirred."[2]

---

2. It's a James Bond thing.

ETHICS? WHAT ARE THOSE?

I'll admit it. This book is steeped in treachery, lies, and deception.[1] Look, a spy *has* to deceive other people. It's even in the job description: "Spy—a person who secretly collects information on an enemy or competitor." (One former agent told me that a three-word motto for his job was "Befriend and betray.")

In order for a spy to secretly collect information, he or she will use many, many forms of trickery, starting with lying! In fact, you could say that a spy is a *professional liar*. But while you may believe lying is always wrong,

---

1. It's awesome!

sometimes telling a lie can prevent something awful from happening. This means that lying and deception can be necessary—and even good! Here's what I mean:

BAD DECEPTION: A spy who's working for a private agency sneaks his way into a job with a corporation. There he learns of a new, top-secret cure for baldness. The spy steals the formula and sells it to a rival corporation for millions of dollars. Meanwhile, the original inventor of the baldness cure (my hero!) doesn't get a penny.

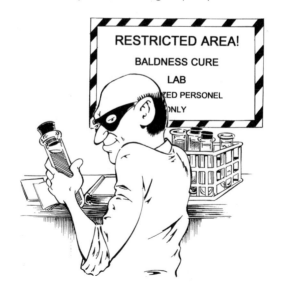

GOOD DECEPTION: Using a secret identity, a government spy sneaks his way into a terrorist group. There he learns of an upcoming attack on his country. He warns the authorities, and the lives of innocent people are saved!

But the lines between bad and good deception are not always so clear. The world of spying can be so tricky and murky, it's been called a "wilderness of mirrors." So that makes having a strong moral sense of right and wrong one of the most important traits of a spy. Of course, "right" and "wrong" can depend on a person's point of view and what country they come from.

During the Revolutionary War, American agent Nathan Hale had a friend who thought spying was disgraceful. Hale said something like this to him: "Anything done for the good of the majority is honorable because it's necessary."

Is that true? When does the *end* (the outcome) justify the *means* (the spying)? Put another way, what makes it okay to do something illegal for the sake of helping a nation?

IMAGINARY CASE IN POINT I

The neighboring nation of Piddlehinton is on good relations with your homeland. But your spymaster informs you that Piddlehinton might have plans to invade your country. If you're willing to go on a mission, you can go to Piddlehinton and steal those invasion plans!

Should you go? Is that the right thing to do?

If you say yes, that means you would be committing a crime of theft against a country that has done no harm to yours. In fact, you'd be stealing something from one of your country's allies.

But let's say you go through with this theft anyway. As you stick the stolen secret invasion plans down your black turtleneck, a security guard shows up. What would you be willing to do to protect the invasion plans?

a. Surrender
b. Try to knock out the guard
c. Use your ninja throwing stars on the guard.

If you chose b or c, you'd be attacking a person who is trying to stop a crime. Uncool!

Of course, we could turn this around. What if a spy from Piddlehinton were trying to steal top secret invasion plans from your country. Remember, this spy would be doing exactly what you were going to do!

Would you try to stop him? Capture him? Throw ninja stars at him?

IMAGINARY CASE IN POINT II

Ooh, I have an even tougher dilemma! Let's say your country and Piddlehinton are at war. But war is hard on everyone, and you've heard that some of the people of Piddlehinton are dying of disease.

Through your spy network, you learn that Piddlehinton agents are smuggling supplies into the country. While investigating, you find a group of women and children that are about to cross the border into Piddlehinton.

At first, this seems okay, but then you notice that all of the children have dolls. You've always been secretly afraid of dolls, so you have an agent take a closer look at them. The agent finds that all of the children's dolls are filled with . . . medicine!

What do you do? On the one hand, this medicine is headed to an enemy country. On the other hand, it will probably be used to help innocent people. Are you going to take the medicine away and arrest a bunch of women and children?

This actually *has* happened before. During the Civil War, secret agents smuggled medicine into the South using dolls. These were sometimes found by Union soldiers, who had to decide what to do with the dolls. (Playing with them was not an option).

Do you see how complex the world of spying can be? It's a *big* complex world, too, because every single nation has spies. Even Vatican City, a country with fewer than 1,000 citizens, has at least one spy!

Nations usually send their spies to both friendly and unfriendly countries. That's because a friendly country might have better secrets than an enemy. And there is always the chance that a friendly country might become an *unfriendly* one . . . so, better safe than sorry!

The United States and many other nations have secret agents in every *other* nation in the world. And all US agents have permission to spy wherever they are, *except* for the American agents in Great Britain, Canada, New Zealand, and Australia. These countries (and the United States) are known as the Five Eyes allies, and they have a "you don't spy on us, we don't spy on you" agreement with each other.

IT'S A TRICKY PROBLEM!

It's hard to prove that friendly countries really aren't spying on each other. As one agent said, "How would you verify it—by spying?"

Most nations in the world accept the fact that CIA agents are running around in their country. And in many cases, they're happy to have the spies! That's because CIA agents might find out some good information and then *share* it with those countries. The United States often returns the favor by allowing foreign spies within its borders.

OUR ROLE MODEL: SIR FRANCIS WALSINGHAM

Is it even possible to be a good person and also a good spy? Maybe. Sir Francis Walsingham (c. 1530-1590) created England's first spy agency. In his 20 years of leading a team of more than 70 secret agents, Walsingham protected Queen Elizabeth from assassins and England from invasion by Spain.

In all the time Walsingham ran the spy agency, he never once used it for his own benefit. In fact, Walsingham paid his spies himself, out of his own pocket. (Trust me, that's impressive.) So, although Sir Francis Walsingham cheated, lied, and spied for his nation, he was actually an honest man!

Even in the world of spying, there are some rules. And that brings us to *traitors*. A traitor is someone who betrays their own country. This usually involves selling secrets for money, but not always. For example, what do we call a person who gives away important secrets to the *public*? If it is for the public's good, that person is called a "whistle-blower."

But it's not always clear who is a whistle-blower and who is a traitor. For example, in 2010, a US Army intelligence analyst named Bradley Manning made a secret video available to the public. The video showed the crews of two American attack helicopters firing at a group of mostly unarmed people in Iraq. (Eleven people were killed in the attack, including a news photographer.)

Manning gave this video and thousands of secret messages to a public website where everyone could see them. Some people thought that made Manning a traitor. Others thought the analyst was a heroic whistleblower. Or was Manning something in between? (After being arrested and sentenced to 35 years for leaking secret information, Manning was released after serving seven.)

In 2013, a US intelligence analyst named Edward Snowden downloaded about 1.7 million documents from classified government files. Wow! This was probably the biggest theft of US military secrets in history. Snowden released many of them to journalists, and others showed up online. The documents revealed secrets about US intelligence operations, and showed how US citizens are sometimes watched by their own intelligence agencies.

Like Manning, Snowden thought of himself as a whistle-blower. Unlike Manning, Snowden fled the United States, and is currently living in Russia.

NOT OUR ROLE MODEL

From the early 1970s to 2007, Monzer al-Kassar was the man to see for anyone looking for guns or explosives. It didn't matter who you were or what you wanted the weapons for—if you had money, al-Kassar would sell them to you.

When asked how he could work with hostile spies, terrorists, and criminals, Kassar answered, "How do I know who's good and who's bad? The bad people for you may be the good people for me."

Hoo-boy. It's pretty clear that Monzer al-Kassar was bad for almost everybody!

CYBERESPIONAGE!

> There's a war out there, old friend, a world war. And it's not about who has the most bullets. It's about who controls the information.
>
> —from the film *Sneakers*

Espionage (pronounced ESS-pee-uh-nahj) means "spying" or "gathering intelligence." It's a very cool word, so use it as much as possible.

So *cyberespionage* is what happens when people use computers to spy.

As I sat down at my desk, I wondered: "How does cyberespionage apply to most people?"

Then I typed in my password to log on to the computer.

Wow, I must have taken some Vitamin Duh this morning!

Cyberespionage!

Cyberespionage affects *everyone*, whether they have a computer or not. And it especially affects Americans. In recent years, the United States has been the victim of over *half* of the world's cyberespionage attacks.

For protection from these attacks, you use passwords. But sadly, many people pick passwords so lame, any toddler could figure them out!

Here's what I mean. This is one of the most popular computer passwords of all time:

Do you see that? It's the word *password* spelled backwards. Wow! This is even cleverer than just using the word *password* for a password. And guess what? Whether spelled backward or forward, *password* is one of the most popular passwords around!

MY ENEMY CAYLA

Germany outlawed the talking My Friend Cayla doll in 2017. The problem was that the doll had a computer that connected to the Internet.

Many "connected" toys like Cayla have cameras and microphones. That makes them perfect tools for spying! And it explains why Germany labeled My Friend Cayla as an "illegal espionage device."

Researchers have found that easy passwords like *dragon, hello,* and *trustno1* are popular choices. Here are some of the most common bad passwords:

PASSWORD1: Oh, that's *much* better than just "password."

123456: Three percent of all computer users use this or another series of numbers for their password.

000000: So simple my cat could type this (in fact, she does all the time).

123123: Still a snap to crack. Still a snap to crack.

654321: Backwards thinking.

ILOVEYOU: Very sweet, but this should really just read "ilovegettinghacked."

ABCDEF: Or any similar letter sequence.

ABC123: Ooh! Getting tricky!

[PERSON'S FIRST NAME]: Because it's so simple, no one will figure it out! (Unless they try.)

Cyberespionage!

PRINCESS: Your prince is coming . . . to hack your computer!

QWERTY: Look where these five letters are placed on a keyboard.

11111: I just threw my head back and laughed.

SHADOW: Yep, it's just me and my shadow (and the hackers!).

GOOGLE: I can't . . .

MICROSOFT123: Let's see if I can guess your Adobe password.

LETMEIN: Let *all* of us in.

ADMIN: You deserve to be fired.

TIGGER: Hey, don't look at me—I'm just reporting this stuff as I see it!

Come on. As a spy, you owe it to yourself to have a better password than *tigger*. For starters, your password should be at least eight characters. And *tigger* is only one character! (That's a joke.)

You shouldn't use actual words in your password. But they can help you pick one. Just take a long word or phrase and substitute in random elements. Symbols like * or @ make a password thousands of times more difficult to hack. For example, *I love espionage* could become *1L*0v3E$piON&4j3*.

But if you think I'm going to help you *steal* passwords, think again. Oh wait, this *is* a book about spying, isn't it? So maybe you should know these strategies so you can protect *yourself* from password theft!

PASSWORD THEFT

One of the best ways to snag someone's password is to just *look* while a person logs on to their computer.

I'm kidding—and I'm not. Try to find innocent reasons to loiter around a person's computer when they log on. The key is that the first few times you do this, make it clear that you're not looking at what the person is doing. But over time, you'll be able to sneak a peek at the keystrokes of the password. Just try to get one keystroke (p!), and then make a note of it. Skip a day, then try to get another keystroke to their password on your next try!

Naturally, you're not going to learn the whole password quickly. This could take years! Maybe even weeks. But with patience, you'll get there. Agents call this the Elephant Technique because it requires patience. (Its name is taken from an old joke.[1])

HOT TIP

To protect yourself from just this sort of thing, try to have a password that takes two hands to type. (It's harder for spies to track all ten fingers.) And if anyone makes a point of hanging around while you're logging on, have your pet elephant step on them.

---

1. Q. How do you eat a whole elephant? A. One bite at a time.

HACKING, COMPUTER ESPIONAGE, AND CYBERWAR

You know what? The Elephant Technique sounds like a ton of work. Maybe you should just *hire* a hacker instead! Because when it comes to computer espionage, there are millions of professional hackers out there trying to sneak into computers all over the planet. For example, a US military officer working in the Pentagon can get up to 5,000 hack attempts on their computer in *one* day.

If enemy hackers succeed even once, the effect can be dramatic. In 2007, Israel's leaders were suspicious of a secret nuclear plant that Israel's enemy, Syria, was building. But Israel's military couldn't just fly jets in and bomb the plant. Syria has really good radar and an air defense that could shoot down Israel's jets.

Instead, Israel's hackers took over the computers that ran Syria's air defenses. The hackers programmed the air defense computers to show that everything was normal and just fine. And *then* Israel flew its jets in and blew up the nuclear plant!

What a fun story! Now, enjoy reading about some of the different ways that high-tech hackers make trouble.

CYBERESPIONAGE: Sneaking on to a computer to *steal* information.

Example 1: In 2017, it was revealed that a Yahoo hack had affected *three billion* people. That's more than a third of all the people in the world! And the "bad guys" had names, e-mail addresses, phone numbers *and* passwords. This is the current record holder for the biggest hack in the world.

Example 2: In 2015, an NSA worker made a *big* mistake. He thought his personal computer was safe because it had the best antivirus software. So he used his home PC to store information on America's secret defenses against cyberattacks.

But the NSA worker's PC was hacked. Afterwards, investigators discovered that his computer's antivirus software was made in *Russia*—and it was actually *spying* software.

Oh, and also? Nobody even noticed the hack for a full year!

Computer viruses, worms, and spying programs are all called *malware*. In 2017, a group studied malware worldwide. It found the fewest computer infections in Sweden. But in China, 49 percent of the computers had malware!

CYBERSABOTAGE: Trying to sneak into a computer to *destroy* its contents.

Example: Years ago, an unknown troublemaker sprinkled thumb drives around the parking lot of a US military base in Tampa, Florida. Naturally, somebody got curious and picked up one of the thumb drives. ("Gee, I wonder why these are here?")

That person went to a computer on the military base and stuck the thumb drive into a computer. ("Guess I'll find out!") And then the thumb drive infected thousands of military computers with a malware program that screwed up everything. ("Oops!")

CYBERZOMBIES: Hacker-spies can take over a group of computers, combine them into a network, and then command them to send out viruses or commit other mischief. The infected computers are called *zombie computers*. Their network is a *robot network* or *botnet*.

Example: Security experts discovered a Chinese computer espionage group in China nicknamed The

Shadow Network. The experts watched in amazement as the hackers infected computers in over a hundred different countries and turned them into a global network of botnets.

These zombie computers were controlled remotely and reported to servers in China. Among other things, the botnets snuck into India's *most* top secret computers. They stole reports on Indian missile systems and learned military secrets about India's allies, including the United States.

CYBERWARFARE: When two nations go to war in the twenty-first century, the first thing that happens is their *computers* start attacking each other. Because, while it takes time to launch jets and fire missiles, a computer attack can happen at the speed of light!

Example: In 2009, the nations of Georgia and Russia went to war. But before the tanks rolled, Georgia's government computers were attacked. Russian hackers shut down Georgia's media, banking, and government computers.

What the Russians did is called a DDoS (distributed denial of service). That's what happens when an enemy sends millions of fake visitors to a website, causing it to crash. This is a big deal if it's a government website that is crucial for communications.

Russia used cyberwarfare again in 2014, when it attacked Ukraine. Hackers were even able to turn off electricity at power stations. But Russians aren't the only ones who make DDoS attacks. In 2017, almost 30 percent of the world's DDoS attacks came from China. And 22 percent of them came from the United States.

CYBERWARRIORS RULE

To help deal with these problems, there is a branch of the US military defense called the US Cyber Command. Agents working there call themselves *cyberwarriors*, which we can all agree is the coolest job title ever.

What do US cyberwarriors worry about? Russia, yes. And China! Most experts think that China has more cyberwarriors than any other country. Heck, there is even a Chinese university that teaches courses like Network Attack Technology. Another thing the Chinese government does is look for kids who have been caught hacking. Then it hires the hackers!

To keep up, the United States government recruits cyberwarriors. Do *you* want to become one? If so, you should know about the US Cyber Challenge. It's a national talent search for high school cyberwarriors. There is a contest where young hackers compete against each other in cybercompetitions.

KNOW YOUR SPY AGENCIES!

The US Cyber Command (USCYBERCOM) was founded in 2010. Among other things, it's charged with keeping government computers safe from attack.

USCYBERCOM has its own government seal, and on its inner ring is a code reading

9ec4c12949a4f31474f299058ce2b22a

Of course, people tried to decode that, and their guesses were more interesting than the real answer[2]:

★ "If you can read this, send us a job application!"
★ "drowssap."
★ "Access denied."
★ "Made you look!"
★ "Be sure to drink your Ovaltine."
★ "If the intelligence community is a family, think of us as the uncle no one talks about."
★ "In God We Trust. (Everybody else gets monitored.)"
★ "You just got pwned."

---

2. If you e-mail me, I'll tell you what it is.

KNOW YOUR SPY AGENCIES!

You've probably never heard of the biggest US spy agency. That's because the National Security Agency (NSA) is also the most secretive agency. The fact that it even existed was kept secret for its first 20 years! That's why the NSA's nickname is No Such Agency.

The NSA is in charge of making and breaking secret codes and waging "information warfare." It's so big, the NSA measures its computer space in acres. *Acres!* And with its network of supercomputers, the NSA looks for important details in one billion e-mails, phone calls, Twitter feeds, IMs, and texts every *day*.

Ooh, and that means something like this could happen:

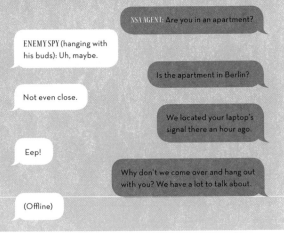

NSA AGENT: Are you in an apartment?

ENEMY SPY (hanging with his buds): Uh, maybe.

Is the apartment in Berlin?

Not even close.

We located your laptop's signal there an hour ago.

Eep!

Why don't we come over and hang out with you? We have a lot to talk about.

(Offline)

One year, the Cyber Challenge was won by a 17-year-old named Michael Coppola. To win, he hacked into the main Cyber Challenge computer and added points to his own score.

Was that cheating? Oh, please! The judges loved it. As Michael said, "It's cheating, but it's like the entire game is cheating." (Something tells me he made a good cyberwarrior.)

MISINFORMATION!

Edward Lansdale was a US agent who came up with an interesting way to confuse opponents: Lansdale would publicly *thank* enemy leaders for their help! This would lead to conversations like this:

ENEMY SOLDIER: How did you help that American spy?
ENEMY LEADER: I didn't!
SOLDIER: Then why did the Americans send a singing

telegram just now, thanking you for your assistance?

LEADER: He is just doing that to make you suspicious of me!

SOLDIER: So you *didn't* help him?

LEADER: No! Of course not!

SOLDIER: Yet I have never known a singing telegram to be wrong . . .

That Edward Lansdale was a tricky one! In fact, *all* spies are tricky.

A man named Peter Ustinov wrote a play about how tricky a spy's life is. In it, a small country named Concordia is caught in a power struggle between the United States and Russia. To survive, Concordia needs to be crafty!

So, to play the two countries against each other, Concordia's spymaster tells the American ambassador that the Russians have broken the secret US code.

"We know they know our code," the American says. "We only give them things we want them to know."

Concordia's spymaster is stunned! He walks to the Russian Embassy and tells their ambassador, "The Americans know you know their code."

The Russian answers, "We have known for some time that the Americans knew we knew their code. We have acted accordingly—by pretending to be fooled."

Amazing! The spymaster then returns to the American

Embassy and tells them, "The Russians know you know they know you know."

"What?" the American ambassador says in surprise. "Are you sure?"

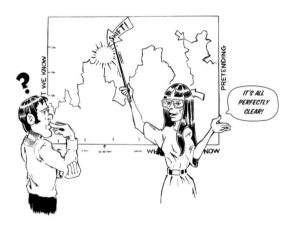

But here's how crazy the world of spymasters is. There is no way to tell if the American ambassador was only *pretending* to be surprised!

This kind of tricky deception can be called *misinformation*. Misinformation is a lie intended to trick a person into thinking that fiction is fact. And once the mistake has been made, the result can be disastrous.

MISINFORMATION: THE SAMURAI WAY!

The Taira and Minamoto clans were two warring factions in medieval Japan. During a battle, the Taira sent a small group of their best samurai fighters to the front line. These fighters challenged the Minamoto to do likewise. The proposal was that only the elite samurai would battle to the death. In this way, fewer people would fight and lives could be saved.

The Minamoto agreed to this idea, and they watched with great interest as their handpicked samurai fought for the clan's honor. What the Minamoto *didn't* see was the army of Taira warriors creeping up behind them. And then the Minamoto samurai had their heads cut off their bodies by those misinforming, sneaky Taira warriors!

Here's another case where a little misinformation had colossal consequences. About 200 years ago, Napoléon Bonaparte ruled France. But he wanted more power! To help make himself look good and his opponents look bad, Napoléon had his spies forge a document supposedly written by the ruler of Russia, Peter the Great. In it, the fake Peter said that he wanted to conquer the world. Naturally, the world was very concerned about this! So to protect everyone from the big, bad Russian,

Napoléon kindly stepped in to save the day. (Then Napoléon tried to conquer the world himself.)

Adolf Hitler used misinformation when he created an excuse to invade Poland. In 1939, German spies faked a Polish attack on a German radio station near the Poland/ Germany border. Operation Canned Goods involved German intelligence agents dressed in Polish uniforms entering the radio station. The fake Poles took over the radio microphone, gave a short speech encouraging Poland to attack Germany, fired a few shots, and left.

Even though the whole thing was bogus, it gave Germany the excuse it needed to invade Poland. On September 1, 1939, German troops crossed the border, and World War II was underway.

These are all cases where confusion agents and misinformation worked. But that kind of thing should be almost impossible today. I mean, fact-checking on the Internet is so simple! You could just go to FactCheck.org or Snopes.com to find out if something is real.

Yet, somehow, spreading misinformation is more popular than ever. All a person or group has to do is lie, lie, lie. And then lie some more! The key is to repeat the misinformation over and over in a variety of ways.

For example, think of *memes*. We all know that memes are supposed to be funny or clever or eye catching. Although memes are not places to get facts or news, they are very popular. So even if they contain lies, there's always *someone* who believes what the memes say without really thinking about it!

And it's not just memes that are to blame. Tweets, forwarded e-mails, blogs, videos, and even text messages can contain lies.

And that brings us to . . .

THE MOST SUCCESSFUL SPY MISSION IN HISTORY

Michael Hayden is an American who was the head of both the CIA and the NSA. So he knows his spy stuff! And Hayden says that the most successful spy operation in world history took place in 2016.

That was the year the Russian government hacked the US presidential election.

There were two main groups trying to win that election: the Republican Party and the Democratic Party. But before the Americans could vote, Russian hackers snuck onto the computers of the Democratic leaders. They hacked 19,000 e-mails and shared them online. Then another 58,000 e-mails were shared.

That's a lot of hacked e-mails! Most of them were boring, like newsletters and recipes and stuff. But some e-mails were embarrassing for the Democratic leaders. And according to the experts at places like the CIA, NSA, and FBI, that was what the Russians wanted.

By weakening the most powerful democracy on Earth, the Russians were hoping to make themselves stronger. So they were being "online confusion agents"!

BUT WAIT—THERE'S MORE!

Have you ever gone to a website, then clicked somewhere else and seen an ad for something you were looking at a few minutes before? Technology companies are very good at tracking your online moves. And so were the Russian hackers in 2016. They used Facebook and Google to anonymously send thousands of misleading ads, memes, and social media pages to Americans. That was pretty sly! Although they didn't realize it, anyone who forwarded or shared this misinformation helped spread the Russian message. Hackers also sent out floods of tweets with false information. For example, just before Election Day, helpful tweets told people they could save time by voting by text. Of course this was untrue.

Is there a way to *prove* that Russia's 2016 hacking and misinformation changed the election's outcome? No. But did it *affect* the presidential election? Absolutely!

This is a problem that will become more critical each year. I mean, think about American voting machines. They use software to keep track of voters and tally results. These machines *will be* hacked in the future—unless cyberwarriors are there to stop it.

SPYING THE DIFFERENCE BETWEEN FACT AND FICTION

WHERE DID THIS MESSAGE/ARTICLE/INTEL COME FROM?

★ Is it from a respected news site? ☺
★ Was it clickbait at a website? ☹
★ Did it show up in your social media newsfeed?
★ Did someone send it to you? Who?
★ Are you sure this isn't from a satire site, like the *Onion* or *Mad* magazine?
★ Does the site have an "About Us" section you can read?

WHAT'S THE DOMAIN NAME OF THE WEBSITE THE INTEL CAME FROM?

★ If it ends in .gov or .org or .com that's *much* better than something like .com.co. or .ru.

SO WHAT CAN WE DO?

Everyone needs to think like spies! That's the best way to catch online confusion agents. And *that* means we have to ask questions about our intel (what spies call information).

Is the intel from a reliable website? Or is it coming

WHAT'S *IN* THE INTEL?

* ★ Is someone helped or hurt by this message?
* ★ Are facts backed up by quotes and sources, or are they just opinions?
* ★ Does the message have spelling errors, grammar problems, or ALL CAPS? (If so, that's really suspicious.)
* ★ Who is the intended audience?

FINAL STEP

* ★ Check any claims the intel makes at a good news site or fact-checking website (like FactCheck.org, International Fact-Checking Network, PolitiFact.com, and Snopes.com).

from a meme or forwarded e-mail or Facebook site that might be spreading false gossip?

Bad intel (like misinformation) gets *bad results*. So don't share any intel that you think might be untrue. A man named Fred Yannantuono wrote a palindrome (something spelled the same backwards and forwards) about this. The palindrome is called "How Rumors Spread":

Idiot to idiot to idiot to idiot to idiot to idi...

Ouch! But it shows that if you want the truth, you have to work for it. As the leader of the fact-checking site Snopes.com said, "When you're looking at truth versus gossip, truth doesn't stand a chance." But truth only loses if people *don't* think.

Now, speaking of computer crimes, did someone smear peanut butter on my keyboard? It feels gooey. Yuck! And although I cannot prove anything, I suspect Russian involvement.

SECRET AGENT TOOL KITS AND SELF-DEFENSE!

Hey, you're still here? Just hang on a second while I put my customized Swiss Army knife down. It isn't just *any* pocketknife. In addition to the usual attachments (retractable ballpoint pen, wrench, flashlight), it has a memory chip that self-destructs if anyone tampers with it.

The pocketknife also has fingerprint identification with a heat sensor—so the memory chip only works while my finger's *attached* to my body. If an enemy agent cuts off my finger and tries to use it, my memory chip would self-destruct!

Of course, if someone cut my finger off, I probably wouldn't be that worried about my memory chip.[1]

Anyway, this chapter is about the things a spy should keep in his or her tool kit. One thing a spy *shouldn't* have in there is a joke book. Spies do not joke around! That's because they are often in tense situations that aren't very funny.

Worse, spies often have to work in tense *nations* that aren't very funny. You know, the kind of countries that have traditions of mean dictators, ruthless police officers, and really bad television shows. These are the type of countries that might have jokes like this one from Russia. It's a joke about people who tell jokes:

There are people who *tell* jokes. Then there are people who *collect* jokes. And finally, there are people who *collect* the people who *tell* jokes.

---

1. On the plus side, clipping my nails wouldn't take as long!

Heheh . . . ouch.

Now picture this real-life situation:

A Russian agent enters a Moscow movie theater. The theater is showing the premiere of a Hollywood blockbuster. As the film starts, the Russian puts on the coolest spy gadget that's ever been created—night-vision goggles!

As the agent looks around, it's pretty clear he isn't interested in watching the movie. Nope, he's trying to catch a *pirate*.

Ah-ha! Our agent's night vision reveals that someone is videotaping the screen—in other words, a criminal is making a movie of the movie! This is known as a pirated copy, and while it might make a *lot* of money for the movie pirates, it will also cost the movie studio millions of dollars in lost sales.

In this case, the movie being pirated was one of that endless series of Pirates of the Caribbean films. Disney hired a private spy agency to take care of just this sort of problem. (This particular agency is run by retired Russian intelligence officers and policemen.)

So with his night-vision goggles, the agent caught a pirate making a pirated version of a pirate movie!

Hey, speaking of movies, have you ever heard an actor say, "This is a crazy idea, but it just might work"? It turns out there's a US government agency devoted to *exactly* that kind of approach to inventing things. It's known as . . .

THE DEPARTMENT OF MAD SCIENTISTS!

Okay, the department's official name is the Defense Advanced Research Projects Agency (DARPA), but its nickname is more accurate. After all, according to DARPA's director, the people working there are an "elite army of futuristic techno geeks." When DARPA was originally created, its mission was to prevent the United States from ever being surprised by a cool invention that another country was working on. So DARPA is constantly looking for scientists doing things so surprising and crazy, nobody else will believe in them.

What kinds of surprises? Well, most of them are secret, but here are a few things the mad scientists have invented:

- ★ the computer mouse
- ★ video conferencing
- ★ GPS systems for navigation, like Google Maps
- ★ stealth jets that radar can't detect
- ★ language translators
- ★ voice recognition technology, like Siri
- ★ self-driving cars
- ★ artificial limbs that look and act like real ones

You've definitely heard of another one of DARPA's inventions: the Internet! Yep, back in the 1970s, the Net was a project designed to help with military communication. And here's the beauty of DARPA's mad scientists: they share their inventions whenever they can. Whenever DARPA comes up with an invention that will help society, they *give it away*. So, we *all* get to use the Internet.

Thanks, DARPA!

Before I share more information about gizmos and technology, I have to tell you about the *Moscow Rules*. These are rules that CIA agents came up with while working in Moscow, which used to be the hardest place in the world to do some good spying. One of the Moscow Rules is this: "Technology will always let you down."[2]

If you've ever had a computer or a Swiss Army knife freeze up on you, you know what that means. And that's why a good spy knows there is no substitute for human intelligence, or HUMINT.

There are also useful low-tech supplies for gathering intel. Check around and see if you have any or most of these:

- ❏ Sunglasses: Wraparounds or mirrored pilot glasses are the spy's preferred models.
- ❏ Lockpicking device: Also known as a bent paper clip.

---

2. Other Moscow Rules include, "Any operation can be cancelled" and "Moscow is really cold."

Secret Agent Tool Kits and Self-Defense!

- ❏ Old cell phone: Save your cell phones. With a battery and a chip, they are the perfect way to store important numbers or messages. (Remember, you can write things in the address bars). And you can easily hide something like a note inside a cell phone, even if it doesn't have a battery or chip!
- ❏ Binoculars or mini telescope: I don't have to explain this, do I?
- ❏ Camera: In the old days of film, special cameras could take a picture of a whole page of secret information and then reduce it on film to the size of a dot. These were called microdot cameras. Since everyone knows about these, get a polka-dot camera, and catch your enemies unaware! (But also, use your cell phone's camera as a backup.)
- ❏ Dabs of wax (or chewing gum): One of the easiest ways to steal a paper is to dab the back of a clipboard or folder with bits of modeling clay or magician's wax. As you're walking and talking, casually set your clipboard down on the document you want. Then pick it up!
- ❏ Fake coins: Spies have been known to keep poisonous suicide pills in hollow coins. That way, if captured, a really dedicated spy can end his life before he's tortured into giving away a national secret. I do something similar: I carry Flintstones

vitamins with me in a special container. If I'm captured, I will immediately eat one so that the vitamin gives me courage.

While these supplies are all well and good, how do you carry all of them around? Many agents wear cargo pants and also a sport jacket or large shirt that they customize with additional pockets. And check out this coat:

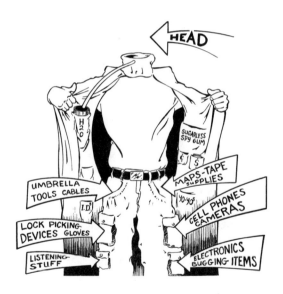

WEAPONS AND SELF-DEFENSE!

Because of your dangerous profession, the time may come when you have to defend yourself. But even though spies don't like to attract attention, defending yourself can be a noisy business. For instance, I go into a karate crouch if attacked. Next, I freak my adversary out by screaming, "Hiiiiiyaaaa!" And then I run away—fast.

Even louder than my martial arts screech is the "crack!" of a gun when it fires. (This sound is partly from the bullet breaking the sound barrier.) The need for a quieter gun led US agents during World War II to invent a barrel to fit over the end of a .22 pistol. Its purpose was to muffle the sound of the gun . . . so, it was one of the first silencers!

Although very useful, a silencer limits a gun's power and accuracy. To get around this problem, British agents in the 1970s came up with a retro-weapon—a small, powerful crossbow that shot a short arrow (called a *bolt*). It could also shoot knife blades, which is pretty awesome!

Wait, I know what you're thinking: "But there are all *sorts* of silent weapons that spies could use, like daggers, tree twigs, and thermonuclear devices." And you're right! But the problem with these weapons is that while they may be silent, the *victim* will make noise while you're using them! For example, have you ever been stabbed with a thermonuclear device? I have, and it hurt so much I had to use my defensive screech: "Aaaayiiiiih!"

In search of the most silent weapon of all, the US Army developed a special poison dart gun.[3] Its dart was just slightly wider than a human hair. This made the dart almost impossible to detect, and the victim might not even notice he'd been shot until after he was dead.

THE TOUGHEST SPIES AROUND

Israel is a tiny country surrounded by nations that would like to destroy it. That means Israel's international spy agency, Mossad, stays busy! The agency employs very few people. So Mossad's agents often see many dangerous operations, and they are considered by many the toughest spies around.[4] There's even a joke about this:

An enemy commander was told that there's a Mossad spy hiding on the other side of a sand dune.

"Ha!" the commander thought. "That Mossad agent is history!" And so he sent his entire platoon over the dune to get the agent.

Thirty minutes later, a lone soldier returned, nursing a knife wound.

"What happened?" sputtered his commander.

"It was a trap, sir," the soldier answered. "There were two of them."

---

3. The dart gun had a very silly name: the "nondiscernible bioinoculator."
4. Secrecy is another hallmark of Mossad. In fact, until 1996, no one even knew who the head of the agency was!

Of course, secret agents aren't usually out to hurt or kill people. It would be more convenient if enemy guards just had an off switch, but in my experience, these switches are really hard to locate. And despite what you see in spy movies, knocking someone out isn't easy. But if an agent had to knock a guard cold, he'd choose what's known as a *blackjack* (a.k.a. a cosh or sap). This is a short club that has a heavy metal center, usually lead. That metal center is wrapped in leather, heavy cloth, or foam.

The idea is that as the blackjack hits someone on the head, the power of the hit will spread out a little. So the blackjack is less likely to break bones or cause bleeding than a hard wooden or metal club without padding. Even so, I think the safest way to dispatch your enemies is with a foam noodle. Sure, it will take more swings to get them to surrender, but safety first!

What other kinds of hidden weapons might enemy agents be using? To find out, I visited the website of the US Transportation Security Administration (TSA). It's in charge of keeping air travel safe, and it lists items that cannot be taken aboard an aircraft. Things like:

★ Meat cleavers
★ Spear guns
★ Swords
★ Cattle prods

★ Brass knuckles
★ Nunchakus
★ Throwing stars

Fun Fact: Until recently, snow globes were also forbidden on planes—"even with documentation"!

Just now, I was wondering how many regular citizens are walking around out there with concealed weapons like snow globes or handguns. Let's see . . . it looks like over 1.3 million people in Florida alone have permits to carry hidden guns. In that case, I'll have my spy agency equip me with a variety of devices. No, not firearms. Guns are for wussies! The genius of my hidden weapons items lies in the fact that no one would ever be suspicious of *any* of them.

And this brings me to the Worst Concealed Weapon Ever. Believe it or not, the KGB (Russia's old secret service agency) developed a weapon called the rectal pistol. It was a small suppository (think of a gel tab someone might take for a headache) that an agent would hide up his . . . er, you know. Anyway, after retrieving the little tube, the single-shot canister would fire a 4.5 mm bullet if its barrel were rotated. (Imagine if it went off while the agent was hiding it!)

Speaking of Russian spies,[5] one was once caught in Germany with an interesting lipstick container. You see, it contained a bullet that could be shot out the container's "barrel"! Nicknamed the "Kiss of Death," the lipstick pistol was a good example of how spy gadgets can be built into ordinary-looking items.

Not to be outdone, the CIA came up with its own single-shot device: a tube of toothpaste nicknamed the "Stinger." This has always made me wonder if a tired CIA

---

5. For most of the twentieth century, Russia was known as the Soviet Union (or the Union of Soviet Socialist Republics, or just USSR). This particular agent was a *Soviet*. But to keep things simple, this book will always use the words *Russia* and *Russian*.

agent ever checked into a hotel, then flossed and got ready to brush his teeth . . . and *bang*!

There are also really high-tech weapons for self-defense. For starters, you already know what a Taser is. It's a great tool for when you need to take out an enemy spy or out-of-control lacrosse coach. But what if you're being attacked by a whole *squad* of lacrosse coaches?

What you need is the Taser Shockwave Barrier! (It's real.) The TSB fires two dozen electrified probes, all in the same direction. There's no escaping its shockwave barrier! Plus, it gets you out of lacrosse practice.

Another thing I've always wanted is what's called an Active Denial System (ADS). The ADS fires a beam, and when it hits an enemy agent, she feels like her skin is burning. But it isn't! Yet it still makes the agent *think* her skin is on fire, and nobody can stay in the beam for more than a few seconds.

The ADS beam only penetrates $1/64$ of an inch into the skin. It's good that it doesn't go any deeper, because nothing stinks worse than an enemy agent engulfed in actual flames. The ADS does have some drawbacks. It's bulky, and if it's stormy outside, the raindrops will break up the beam.

That makes the enemy agent feel warm and refreshed, which probably isn't the response you're hoping for.

MAGIC AND UNMENTIONABLES!

Magicians have influenced many spy gadgets. For example, during World War II, a British magician named Jasper Maskelyne had an idea: Why not use fake tanks to trick the enemy? These props could be made from plywood. As long as they looked realistic to someone flying overhead, they would work!

This idea is still being used today. In fact, I was just looking at some photos of very realistic-looking Russian tanks. Their only drawback is that they're inflatable. All it would take is a nail in a tank's track, and *kaboom!* That tank would pop like a party balloon.

Famous magician and escape artist Harry Houdini had a variety of blades and picks that he'd hide in the heels of his shoes. Houdini also had an oval container full of tools that he could hide in the back of his mouth. These could be used to pick the locks of the chains, chests, and rooms that he was locked in.

Inspired by Houdini, the CIA also invented a small tool kit of lock-picking devices. The tools were hidden in a four-inch capsule that looked like a giant pill. It was called the CIA Escape and Evasion Rectal Suppository. (This makes me very uncomfortable.)

THE GADGET MASTER: CHARLES FRASER-SMITH

In the James Bond stories, the gadget master is known as Q. This character was based on a real intelligence inventor named Charles Fraser-Smith. He was a British researcher who became famous for hiding gadgets; for example, concealing spy cameras in cigarette lighters.

During World War II, the gadget master came up with compasses hidden in coat buttons. To find them, you just unscrewed the top of the button. But the trick was, the compass-buttons unscrewed opposite from the usual way. Fraser-Smith's idea was that Germans were so logical, they would never guess that something might unscrew the wrong way! (And he was right.)

Another challenge for the gadget master was figuring out how to make British agents sneaking into France seem French. To do this, he made garlic-flavored chocolate for the spies to eat. (The idea is that French people have garlic breath.)

As for the Q code name: During World War I, the British had sometimes disguised their warships as regular cargo ships. These concealed destroyers were known as Q-ships. After that, the letter Q came to signify any hidden meaning . . . or any wolf in sheep's clothing! So a Q-tricycle would be a beat-up looking average trike that is actually light, fast . . . and equipped with razor-sharp wheels!

We can see that spying *tactics* have been the same throughout human history. But spying *technology* keeps getting better and better. It seems like a handy new tech-no-gadget is invented each week. I think you should buy them *all*—and then you can give me your used night-vision goggles!

ESPIONAGE AND COMMUNICATION!

Espionage is a secret, intelligence-gathering activity that leaves no trace. So you might be wondering, "How do I do *that*?"

There are a number of possibilities! Let's say you're into industrial espionage. That means you've been hired to discover the secret products a business is developing. You could get started by hacking into the company's computers and pocket calculators. But here are two better ideas:

1. READ. Reading is the quickest and most reliable way to find out what's going on in the world. Following the news and connecting the dots is very important for

intelligence work. In fact, experts say that 90 percent of what a spy needs to know is already public information. (The other 10 percent is in *this* book.)

In 2010, the FBI arrested 10 undercover Russian spies. Not bad! But many spy experts shook their heads at how wasteful the Russians were. "Why not just have one Russian spy read an American paper every day?" an intelligence agent asked.

To prove this point, a CIA officer once hired five people to write a report on the current state of the US military. The people had *no* access to any top secret material. Instead, they just read newspapers, magazines, and books.

A couple of months later, this group turned in its military report. And when the CIA officer shared it at headquarters, the other spies were astounded at how much good intelligence was in it. In fact, the report was so good, it was classified as secret and hidden away . . . even though all the information in it had been public! That's why lots of librarians end up going into the spy business. (Really.) Librarians are curious, they know how to research, and they're good readers. These are all qualities a good spy should have.

2. TALK TO PEOPLE—IN PERSON! It's easy to fall into the habit of going online for information. But professional spies agree that using *human intelligence* (HUMINT) is the

best way to get the pulse of a situation.

Think of it this way: a reporter might be the only other professional who is as interested in secrets as a spy is. And reporters often use contacts (people with inside information) to get their scoops. How do you get a contact? It can be complicated, but the key is to be trust-worthy. This will be hard for you, because you're natu-rally deceptive. So fake it!

HOT TIP

With HUMINT, it can be tricky figuring out where to have a face-to-face meeting. A restaurant? Too romantic! A public park? Too obvious! I advise using building stair-wells. They're not used much, they don't have bugs, and stairwells are also easy to escape from. (You just run down the stairs!)

Here's a good example of HUMINT. About 2,200 years ago, the Roman Empire was at war with the African city of Carthage. During a truce, a group of Roman officers visited an enemy camp. They brought with them "slaves," who were actually other Roman officers in disguise.

Just to make sure that nobody from Carthage got suspicious, the Romans beat one of their slaves right in front of them! Naturally, nobody paid attention to the Roman slaves as they carefully memorized everything they could about the size and layout of the camp. After the meeting was over, the Romans went home. Then they came back and conquered the camp. (Oh, and the Romans won the war, too.)

DON'T KNOW WHOM TO TRUST? CHOOSE A WOMAN!

The most challenging part of HUMINT is knowing whom to trust. To help you with this, make a list of the most suspicious people you know. That is, people who you suspect might not be very trustworthy. (This could take a while.)

Look over the names. How many of your suspicious people are *women*? My bet is that it's less than half. Most people think of women as being trustworthy. And many spymasters think that women make better spies than men.[1] Here are their arguments:

★ Women have excellent social skills.
★ Studies show that women are better at multitasking (doing more than one thing at the same time) than men. And if there's one thing a spy does, it's multitask!

---

1. This isn't to say that no men are trustworthy. *checking notes* Strike that. No men are trustworthy. Avoid them at all costs!

★ Women know more secrets than men, so they get more practice at learning secrets and then keeping them. They are also less likely to boast and let something important slip out.

★ Mothers know the importance of espionage in keeping track of their kids.

★ Women might be more loyal than men.

SECRET COMMUNICATIONS

Once you start using HUMINT, you'll need to find ways to secretly communicate with your fellow spies and contacts. Yes, you could just send them a tweet from your Twitter account. But what if an enemy agent intercepts it? Do you have any idea of the horrible things they might do to that poor innocent little tweet?

Using other electronic communications might not be the answer either. Spies are often caught because they use cell phones. And if your computer is being monitored, how can you send a message?

There are countless options! For example, most spies learn how to leave rocks and sticks in a pattern that only the trained eye of another spy could possibly read. For example:

Speaking of trained eyes, there was once a German spy with one glass eye. (Hey, that rhymes!) He had his eye custom made with a compartment in the back. There, he would hide microfilm and other information. What an ingenious place to hide information—in his own skull!

There are lots of other nonelectronic signals that you can use to communicate with others. A spy could go out in public scratching the back of her head. Sure, this *looks* like an innocent natural gesture. But it turns out that hardly anyone ever actually scratches or rubs the back of their head! So it's a good tip-off signal for any friendly spies watching that the spy has information to share.

Something as simple as a baseball cap can also carry a hidden message. Is the cap's bill to the front? That might mean "Keep your distance; I'm being watched." Is the bill to the side? Perhaps the agent doesn't want to get a sunburned ear. Another clothing technique could involve shoelaces. It's all in the way the shoelaces are laced!

"Pop quiz in math today."

"Beware: boys' restroom has a clogged toilet."

"Stupid cheap shoelaces!"

DEAD DROPS

Dead drops are spots where a spy leaves cash, messages, or snacks for another spy. These dead drops might be indoors but are most commonly in outdoor locations. Oh, and the items left behind must be camouflaged.

An example: American agents once set up an audio dead drop inside of a tree in a park. They placed a hidden microphone and a recording device completely out of view. Afterward, a spy would walk up to the tree, talk to it, and then walk off, trying not to look insane.

For spies operating in Russia, a Moscow park was the dead-drop spot. At an out-of-the-way location, they placed a custom-made hollow rock with a small computer inside. Spies would approach the rock and wirelessly download or upload information with their own handheld computers. This dead-drop rock system worked like a dream until the stone was discovered in 2006. Up until then, it was a great mix of twenty-first-century technology and the Stone Age!

Secret Toilet Papers! German spies sometimes used a custom hollowed-out toilet paper holder for dead drops.

Please do not confuse a dead-drop spot with a drop-dead spot. These can be fatal. (That's a joke.) And speaking of fatal, spies have used the dead bodies of small animals to hide messages, memory chips, or film. Of course, the dead animal was first stuffed by a taxidermist, but the more disgusting it looked, the better. That's because even an enemy agent is unlikely to pick up a squished squirrel or rotten rat to see what's inside of it!

However, agents found that one problem with hiding secrets inside of dead animals was that cats sometimes ran off with the bodies! To foil the felines, agents began sprinkling their host carcasses with hot chili sauce. The cats (who may have been agents themselves) left the dead animals alone after that.

While we're in the animal kingdom, agents agree that if you need to do some dead drops, you should get a dog. That's because a dog gives you endless excuses to leave the house and then go on odd little trips where you can easily make dead drops and pick up dog dookie. Wait—I guess the dog dookie isn't that helpful, is it?

Or you could follow the example of Chinese spies a thousand years ago. They would write a secret message, seal it in wax, and then swallow it. Within 24 hours, they'd be dropping some secret dookie themselves.

HOW TO DEAD DROP!

Imagine that you're ready to set up your own dead drop. You're going to leave something important (like a doughnut) for your contact at an indoor location. Better yet, imagine that you are leaving a doughnut for yourself! For this dead drop, you'll need a plastic container with a lid (like the ones that hold leftovers in the fridge) and a few strips of Velcro.

Attach one strip of Velcro to the bottom of the plastic container. Now attach the other strip to the underside of a table or desk that is your dead-drop spot. Pop the doughnut into the container and put the lid on. Turn the container upside-down and stick it to the other side of the Velcro strip! If the container doesn't hold, just use more Velcro.

When your contact comes along, he doesn't have to worry about ripping the Velcro apart and making a noise.

All he has to do is quietly pop the lid and let the doughnut fall into his hand. Ta-dah!

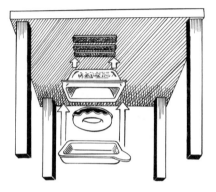

What else? Well, you've probably seen those hide-a-key containers before. These little containers with a magnet can be hidden or stuck to small, out-of-the-way spots. (Agents call these clam dead drops.) And if you have a pond, lake, or stream nearby, consider getting a water-proof pouch that you can hide underwater for a later pickup. Make sure to anchor the pouch under a rock, though. Otherwise, your secrets could float downstream and wash ashore!

BRUSH CONTACTS

The time will come when you need to actually *pass* information to a contact in person. As this is more dangerous than a dead drop, you need to be careful, and practice how to do a brush contact. Here's how:

While walking down a sidewalk or school hallway, you see one of your contacts. If she isn't already expecting to receive something from you, give one of the signals that the two of you already have. This signal should be something subtle, like rubbing your nose or doing the chicken dance.

Now, as you approach each other, put the item you're going to pass in the palm of your left hand. Don't look at each other. As you pass on the right, secretly slip the item into your contact's left hand. This is a thing of beauty when it works, but it looks kind of dumb if one of you drops the item, sort of like a bad baton handoff on a relay team. (And it's even worse if the two agents run into each other!)

SMUGGLING

As you're out on missions, you may need to carry some things with you that you don't want others to know about. One way to disguise the items is with an old, outdated hardcover book. Encyclopedias from the twentieth century are perfect for this. Your best choice is to go to the library and find out when and where they sell old books that are no longer considered useful. These books usually cost less than a dollar; look for a thick old hardcover and buy it.

When you get home, put on some heavy work gloves and get an X-Acto knife. Be careful, an X-Acto blade is sharp—razor sharp. (That's because it *is* a razor!) Better yet, get an adult to use the knife. Now, take a piece of cardboard and slip it into the book about twenty pages before the end. (Trust me.)

Now turn to pages twenty and twenty-one, near the front. Using a pencil, outline a rectangle that is about an inch inside the edges of page twenty-one. Have your adult helper cut deeply along these lines with the X-Acto knife. It might take a bit of cutting to get all the way through to the cardboard at the back end of the book, so carefully push down. Once you've cut a hollow rectangle into your book, trim the edges, recycle the cuttings, and you're in business! You can hide any dastardly item you want in the book, like deviled ham, a digital camera, or digital ham.

Now, why did I have you go to the library to get this book? Because in the history of humankind, nobody has ever looked suspicious carrying a library book!

That book cover makes the perfect cover. Best of all,

your book makes the perfect item for dead drops as well. Just go to the library, make sure your contact sees you, and then leave the book on a shelf. Handoff complete!

A FINAL WARNING ON TRUST

In 1917, there was a revolution in Russia. A new Communist government was set up, and many Russians who feared for their lives fled the country.

Assuming that anyone who had left was an enemy to the new Russia, the Communists created an agency nicknamed the "Trust." Its mission was to persuade the Russians who had run away to *return* home. Using a variety of methods, the Trust did entice a number of former Russians to do just that.

After all, if you can't trust the Trust, whom can you trust? Nobody! Once these Russian emigrants were back, they were usually imprisoned. (Or worse.)

DISHONESTY— IT'S THE BEST SPY POLICY!

Anyone becoming a professional spy knows she's going to have to break some laws. Think about it! That means that since the CIA has about 5,000 full-time spies, it has 5,000 *criminals*.

It sounds bad, but here's one way to look at it: Laws in your country are broken every day by spies from other nations. So it wouldn't be fair if your country's spies didn't do the same thing back![1]

Maybe calling a spy a criminal is too harsh. How about if I describe what spies do as cheating? That still sounds judgmental? There must be a better word! Let's see, I could use *deceive, trick, scam, dupe, hoodwink, double-cross, con, bamboozle, flimflam, sucker, hornswoggle* . . . hmmm, on second thought, *cheating* is just fine.

Anyway, every country has a small army of professional cheaters who are good at sneaking around to get secret information. What kinds of tricks do these rascals use? I'm glad you asked!

TRICKS OF THE TRADE

1. LOOK DUMB! Yes, highly trained spies try to look stupid. That is, spies really *don't* want to look alert, smart, or in any way genius-y. That's because no one thinks a nitwit can come up with a clever plan. And no spy wants to be thought of as clever by the people she's spying on. (This is why I often drool; it lulls people into a false sense of security.) After all, which of these people are you going to be more suspicious of?

---

1. I know, that's a really lame argument. And it's also the one that spies use.

Which is a spy?

Crafty
Professsional

Harmless
Idiot

2. STICK AND MOVE! Another key to trickery is to simply *keep moving*. This is especially useful in social situations. Let's say you sneak into a party to gather information. A suspicious woman comes over to you.

"Who are you?" she asks.

Thinking quickly, you say, "I'm Joe's boss."

"And who is Joe?" the woman continues.

"My employee," you answer. Good one! But you're not going to be able to keep this up much longer, so get *moving*.

"And there he is now!" you add, walking briskly out of the room.

3. GO TO THE RIGHT SCHOOLS! Before World War I, British intelligence agents took classes in the Technique of Being Innocent, the Will to Kill, the Technique of Lying, and something called Dr. McWhirter's Butchery Class. (Yikes!)

Check with your local schools and libraries to see if they have any courses that teach spy skills. If not, ask any neighborhood kids wearing trench coats if they know of any good classes. (Those kids are so suspicious, they have to know *something*.)

4. CHEAP TRICKS ARE BETTER THAN GENIUS PLANS! Don't think that because you're a spy, your plans have to be masterpieces. Sometimes a simple plan is the best plan. For instance, if you need to get someone away from his desk for a moment, tell him that you think you saw his car get hit in the parking lot. Actually, it's even better if you can get someone else (like building security) to pass the word along.

5. GET A KID TO DO YOUR DIRTY WORK! Adults naturally think that all kids are innocent. And kids think that any kid younger than them is also dumber than them. This makes children the perfect accomplices, but only if you can keep them from sticking gum in each other's hair.

6. BE A SMOOTH OPERATOR! British spy Richard Tomlinson once explained the challenges he had to deal with during his training. For one exercise, Tomlinson and his fellow students had to approach a perfect stranger and

DEAR WARLORD: YOU'RE DUMB!

Over 2,000 years ago, a Chinese peasant named Liu Ji worked his way up to being a rebel leader and, eventually, emperor. Not bad! One of Liu Ji's strategies was sending messengers to enemy leaders. The messengers had simple messages, like "You suck!" and "You're a moron!" And these would often enrage the enemy leaders to do stupid things ... like leading their troops into ambushes.

find out the person's name, job, birth date, and passport number.

Tomlinson pretended he was the captain of a yacht and invited two women for a cruise the next day. Since they were going to sail from England to France, Tomlinson told his passengers that he'd need just a *little* information from them: their names, jobs, birth dates, and passport numbers!

It was smart pretending to be the ship's captain. As soon as someone sees you as an expert, you become an *authority figure*. And people don't question authority figures like professors, police officers, or the authors of spy books.

7. DISTRACT A TARGET BY GETTING HER TO TALK ABOUT SOMETHING SHE'S INTERESTED IN! People *love* to talk about themselves ... so, find out what your target's interests are and find a way to work it into the conversation. Let's say

that your target likes to can pickles. Work that into the conversation:

"Canning pickles is one of my favorite hobbies. What's that? You like to can pickles too?"

Now is the perfect time to use flattery:

"I'm sure your pickles are way picklier than mine."

And finally, make some small mistake that gives your target a chance to show off their knowledge:

"As you know, pickles come from cucumbers harvested by fishing boats—Huh? They grow in gardens? Wow, it's lucky that I'm talking to you."

And now you're ready to smoothly pick your person's mind.

"Have you ever noticed that pickles are shaped like nuclear missiles? I wonder how many nuclear missiles *your* country has?"

8. COPY THE CON MEN! Like spies, professional con men are good at tricking people (a.k.a. suckers). Unlike spies, con men then take their money! And a study of these criminals found that con men often follow these two rules:

★ Appeal to a person's greed. Once you know what the target wants, you can easily manipulate him.
★ Try to get your target to do something dishonest. If you can get him to do something wrong, it will be harder for him to ask for help once he's been tricked!

9. HOW MANY TIMES DO I HAVE TO TELL YOU? USE MAGIC! In the 1950s, the CIA hired professional magician John Mulholland to write a manual of trickery and deception for its agents. After all, magicians misdirect an audience's attention and often make things mysteriously disappear. That is pretty similar to a lot of intelligence jobs. There probably isn't a spy out there who wouldn't benefit from having a magician's skills. (Even if I can't think of a practical use for cutting someone in half!)

10. BE CREATIVE! As you're presented with new challenges, keep on exercising your brain to figure out your best approach. For example, during the Revolutionary

THOSE SPYMASTERS WERE MONEY

Benjamin Franklin ran spy networks in France during the American Revolution. That means that the men on the US dollar bill and the hundred-dollar bill were both spymasters!

War, the American spymaster with the code name of Agent 711 was extremely creative. You might know Agent 711 as someone named George Washington.

Washington was so terrific at his job that after the war, the head of the British intelligence operations said, "Washington did not outfight the British, he simply out-spied us." Naturally, George Washington knew that British spies were keeping an eye on his forces. So Washington made his officers and men spread out their camps along the sides of the roads. This sometimes put them miles away from each other, and the soldiers grumbled. But there was a reason for it.

Imagine that it's morning. A British spy in costume is walking along the road when he sees some American soldiers making breakfast. The spy makes a mental note of where they are and then keeps traveling. Over the course of the next five miles, the spy sees groups of American soldiers making their breakfasts the entire way!

The spy then reports that the American army seems to cover five miles—and that made it seem like the army was *much* larger than it actually was! How Agent 711 must have laughed and laughed.

EAVESDROPPING!

As all spies know, a bug is a hidden minimicrophone. And kids love them!

That's because kids know how fun it is to be sneaky. For example, in 1946, a group of Russian schoolchildren gave the people at the US embassy in Moscow a gift. How sweet! It was a carved wooden wall decoration of the Great Seal of the United States.

This gift from the Russian children hung on a wall in the ambassador's home for the next six years. And then a US security team discovered that the carving had a microphone in it. It turned out that Russian agents had been listening in on the ambassador all that time.

Those little brats gave us a bug!

Here's what I love about this story: To solve the bug problem, the United States decided to have a new

ONCE BUGGED, TWICE SHY

US agents sometimes overreact in their search for bugs. During a high-level meeting in Vienna, Austria, two American agents wanted to sweep a meeting room of any bugs. Investigating the room above the meeting area, the agents found a big brass object in the floor. They didn't know what it was, but the thing was suspiciously mysterious!

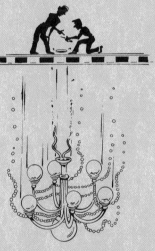

The two agents worked all night with a tool kit to remove the device. When they unscrewed a rod from inside of it, the brass object finally came free! But as they went downstairs, the agents realized they had made a big mistake. The meeting room couldn't be used anymore because the huge antique chandelier in its ceiling had just crashed to the floor and broken into smithereens.

Oops!

Moscow embassy built in 1968. The idea was to carefully watch the Russian workers so they wouldn't try any funny stuff. The problem was the Russians constructed the walls away from the building site, and then trucked them into Moscow. And even worse, the Russians even mixed electronic bugs into the concrete mix for the building.

The result? By the time the new embassy was done, it had so many listening devices, it was just a gigantic radio broadcaster. The United States had to spend $40 million more just to start over. Dang it!

Of course, you don't need technology to eavesdrop. Sometimes you can just be standing right there. Take Mary Elizabeth Bowser. She was a slave owned by Jefferson Davis, the president of the Confederacy during the Civil War. By keeping quiet, Mary was able to gather all sorts of intelligence (especially while serving dinner!), because Davis and his guests assumed she was illiterate.

Burn on them! Mary was born in 1839 as a slave in Virginia. But after being freed by her owners, Mary attended school and received a good education. Because she was both highly intelligent and a good actress, Mary was enlisted as a spy for the Union.

In her role as a spy, Mary pretended to be Ellen Bond, a slow-witted servant who worked at the Confederate White House. And she was treated as if she were invisible! So while doing housework, Mary would read the

EAVESDROPPING TIP!

If you have two cell phones, you can listen in on almost anything. First, set one of the phones to silent. Then go to the area where you want to eavesdrop. Find a place where you can plant the silenced phone. This should be a spot where it won't be noticed but will be out in the open.

Now call the silenced phone and answer it to establish a connection. Set the silenced phone to hands-free or loudspeaker and leave the room!

Take the phone you'll be listening in on to another room. If it has a mute feature, use it, so you can hear through the other cell phone but any noise you make is blocked. If you can't do this, just be quiet!

letters and strategies that were left out in the president's studio. While serving meals, she would listen in on conversations about military strategies and troop movements.

Best of all, Mary had a nearly photographic memory, so she could repeat what she had read and heard word for word!

As the war went on, Jefferson Davis knew there was a leak somewhere in his office or home, but he didn't discover the source until it was too late. It is sad but understandable that after the war was over, the US government destroyed all records relating to its spies in the South, including the ones about Mary. This was done to protect them from revenge. And Mary knew a few things about secrets herself, as she then disappeared entirely from the historical record!

Mary Elizabeth Bowser was one of the most important espionage agents of the Civil War. And remember that she did her best work just by keeping her ears open! Mary taught us the importance of keeping our ears peeled. Sure, it's painful, but that's part of an agent's job.

And now for an inspirational tale of surveillance: Imagine that you're an agent stationed in the tropics. Your boss thinks that enemy forces are using a certain jungle trail, so you have to bug it! To make sure the bug isn't found, you have to hide it in something that will not be a tempting place for the enemy to look. What do you choose?

If you worked for the CIA, you would have picked tiger

BUGS WITH BUGS?

One of the CIA's greatest listening devices was the insect-othopter. This was a remote-controlled fake dragonfly equipped with a tiny motor that a watchmaker made. The flying spy would buzz around and set listening devices outside of windows. The insectothopter worked great, too. But it was so small that if it flew into a breeze it was thrown off course and lost.

Or was it *really* lost?

poop! During the Vietnam War, spy bugs were placed inside real-looking brown clumps. And the bugs inside of the fake bowel movements revealed real enemy troop movements. (There's a joke in there somewhere.)

Okay, let me share a spy tale with a little more class. When Madeleine Albright was the US secretary of state (1997–2001), she had her own particular style. For example, Albright wore jewelry pins that reflected her mood. If things were going well, her pins were butterflies and balloons. Not so good? A spider pin or maybe a snake accessory.

At one point while Albright held office, a sweep of the State Department offices discovered some bugs. Who had planted these listening devices? The Russians! So can you guess what kind of pin Albright wore to her next meeting with the Russians? Yep, a bright bug.

"They got the message," Albright said.

Of course, there have been many times in history when a nation didn't realize that an enemy *could* get its message. For example, at the start of World War I, the Russian army just used regular radio broadcasts to give regular commands. There was no jamming, no codes, no tricks—just orders! Because radios were so new in 1914, the Russians hadn't considered that someone *else* might be listening in.

As a result of this mistake, the Germans wiped out an entire Russian army at the city of Tannenberg.

SURVEILLANCE!

Admit it: you've been secretly observing people for years. How else could you pounce on the last piece of pizza *every* time?

In spy agencies, this is called surveillance, and I'm glad you've already had some practice. A good spy like you can secretly observe an individual, a group, a company, or even an entire nation without anyone knowing it. In fact, I've been secretly watching the country of Liechtenstein since 2015. (Luckily, it's not very big.)

And now, I have a special treat: this is the only surveillance story involving diaper rash that you'll read in your lifetime! In the 1950s, the CIA worked with airplane makers to develop a spy plane called the U-2. It was designed to take high-quality photos from altitudes over 70,000 feet in the air. Back when it was built, that was higher than Russian jets or even missiles could fly. In fact, 70,000 feet up is where outer space begins!

The U-2 flew so high and on such long missions that its pilots had to wear space suits with built-in diapers. As one spy plane pilot said, "I learned the hard way . . . that you can get diaper rash from Gatorade."

In 1962, US spy planes took photos of new missile launching sites in Cuba. But Cuba didn't have the ability to make missiles, so Cuba's ally—Russia—had to be the supplier.

President John F. Kennedy called in a Russian diplomat named Georgi Bolshakov to explain. Bolshakov was outraged! He acted insulted and denied that there were any missiles of *any* kind in Cuba.

YOU DON'T PLAY MUCH BASEBALL IN RUSSIA, DO YOU?

So, the Russian was shown the spy plane photos. "And what do you think those are?" he was asked.

Bolshakov hesitated. Then he smiled and said, "Baseball fields, perhaps?"

Ha! President Kennedy was too polite to do it, but right then he could have shouted, "That's the *second*-worst excuse of all time!" (The worst excuse of all time comes a little later in this chapter.)

Thanks to spy satellites, surveillance has only gotten easier. The first US spy satellite was launched into orbit in 1961. But while those early spy satellites could *take* pictures of the earth below, there was no easy way for us to *get* those photos!

Back then, the spy satellite had to eject its film into a container called a camera pod. Then the pod had to be ejected from the satellite. After plummeting down to the earth, the pod had to be retrieved—sometimes from the other side of the planet. Finally, the film had to be developed, and by then, a lot of time could have passed. In fact, in 1967, there was a conflict known as the Six-Day War—and that war was already finished before satellite photos of it started to come in!

Since the 1970s, digital technology has made it possible for satellites to beam photographs and other information back to Earth. If you've used Google Earth, you know there are swarms of satellites circling the planet and beaming pictures down to it. That's a lot more convenient, and it means that today, *anyone* could be under observation at any time.

But even though spy satellites can spot an individual person, they still can't track that last piece of pizza. So keep your eyes open!

FREEZE-FRAME!

To get more specific photos, spies have hidden remote-controlled cameras inside things like neckties, cigarette cartons, gloves, eyeglass cases, thermoses, watches, belts, glue sticks, and even *cuckoo clocks*. But as a beginner, you should just practice being sneaky with a cell phone camera. Follow these tips:

★ Change the settings so that the phone won't auto-matically flash or make sounds. Nothing is worse than setting up the perfect stealth shot and then giving yourself away with a loud *beeep!*

★ Practice taking pictures while holding the camera at your waist without looking through the screen. Try not looking right at your target. Experiment with different wrist angles.

★ Once you are decent at shooting from the hip, try doing it while hiding your phone with your body or a long-sleeved T-shirt, sweater, or coat. (The idea here is to cover the screen but not the lens.)

★ If you think you've been spotted, try turning or moving away from the target while still snapping pictures.

TALKING TRASH

Surveillance isn't all glamorous hip-shooting and cuckoo clocks. Sometimes you're going to have to roll up your sleeves and get dirty! Going through a subject's trash

SPIES ARE LOOKING AT YOUR ONLINE PHOTOS!

Innocent bystanders can gather important intelligence without realizing it. Imagine a tourist in Paris. She is trying to get a shot of her Aunt Ruby by the Eiffel Tower, but just as she snaps the photo, foreign agents steal it. No, not the picture—they steal the Eiffel Tower! But just as the criminals commit their very unrealistic crime—*click*—the tourist photographs them.

Regular people really do take pictures of top secret things all the time without realizing it. Professional spies call these kinds of photos Aunt Minnies because some-one's aunt (or other relative) is often in the picture.

And that's why intelligence agents are online and looking through people's Facebook photos right now. (Seriously.) This job used to be a lot more difficult. During World War II, US agents were sent out on missions to antique stores. There, they would look through photo albums, trying to find good Aunt Minnies. (Seriously!)

AUNT RUBY IN AN AUNT MINNY

is a great way to find evidence of what she's been up to. But don't actually *take* the person's trash away. That would be stealing! (It really is.) However, it's legal to go through any garbage that's been set out on the sidewalk or in a dumpster.

Of course, it looks a little suspicious if you're seen going through someone's garbage bags. Back in 1991, a police officer spotted two men doing just that in Houston, Texas. The men were searching the trash of a technology company bigwig. And it turned out the men worked for the French government. *Sacré bleu!*

This led the French embassy to release *the worst spying excuse of all time*: Yes, the trash collectors were employees of the French government. But, no, they weren't spying! Instead, the men were "collecting grass cuttings to use as fertilizer in the French embassy's garden."

They should have used that excuse in the garden instead, because it was pure bull manure!

Big candy companies spy on each other all the time. During one of Nestlé's spy campaigns against Mars, Incorporated, agents went dumpster diving outside the Mars headquarters for months. To make sure nobody noticed the missing garbage bags, the agents replaced them with *different* bags of trash.

Then the Nestlé agents had to sort through the bags they had taken. Inside were coffee grounds, shredded

GARBAGE TIME

When double-agent Aldrich Ames came under suspicion, FBI agents went through all of his trash every week and then put it all back the way it was for nearly a full year.

documents covered in food, and even underwear. (*Blech!*) The spies had to be tough because their job was to take those soggy pieces of shredded documents and patch them back together. There's no way to sugar-coat it—that's the worst spy job I've ever heard of!

Now let's set our surveillance sights a little higher. Did you know that there are a number of small model helicopters and planes that can be fitted with cameras? Of these devices, my favorite is one that falls off of maple trees.

Or at least the *device* looks like it fell off a maple tree. Students at the University of Maryland invented what they call the "world's smallest controllable single-winged rotocraft." This microvehicle looks like a maple seed and isn't much bigger. If you've ever seen a maple seed fall, you know that it has a unique spiral flight due to the "wing" attached to the seed. This camera-fitted rotocraft uses that same movement to take off from the ground and hover. Or you can just hold it in your hand and toss it into the air!

COMINGS AND GOINGS: THE STAKEOUT!

Keeping track of *where* your target is and *when* they are there can be tricky. Let's say you need to know when a particular person drives away from a certain place. You could stake out her location, but that might take five minutes . . . or longer!

If you have a cheap wristwatch, simply wrap it in duct tape. Then slyly stick it underneath one of the car's tires that is closest to the curb. At some point, the person will drive off, running over the watch. Later, you can come back and grab it, and the time the hands stopped on the watch is the time your person drove away.

Oops, you didn't use a digital watch, did you? That won't work for this technique! And neither will larger timepieces that might be spotted by the driver.

BE A FOLLOWER!

If you're ever assigned to put a tail on someone, don't sweat it. The more nervous you are as you follow your target, the more likely it is you'll get spotted. And remember, it's not the end of the world if you get discovered. Unless, that is, a spy delivers the plans for the Ultimate Death Machine to some evil genius. (In that case, it *is* the end of the world, and thanks for nothing.)

If you're tracking someone who *might* be suspicious, you don't want to constantly be behind him. Instead, get in front of him! Whether from the front or behind, try to get into the walking rhythm of your target. Concentrate on his movements and move in harmony with him . . . but be careful. If you get too tuned in to his movements, the two of you may break into a song-and-dance number!

You'll probably have some idea of where your person is headed, so walk ahead and then stop at a choke point—for example, a spot where lots of people are going in and out of a building—and see where your target is.

Now stay alert!

★ Don't make sudden movements as you work. If you're diving into doorways, everyone will notice you.

★ Don't move your whole head when tracking your target. From a distance, he'll be able to see this. Instead, use just your eyes to look near your target, but avoid making eye contact with him. If you can, follow your target's progress by watching his reflection in windows.

★ Most importantly, never make eye contact with your target! As soon as you do this, you might as well give up. Because even if the person doesn't recognize you, he will probably remember you if he sees you again! (This is especially true if your target is one of your parents.)

That's one reason why following a target is best done with at least one other person. If you have a partner, a hands-free cell phone works great for communication. And if one person gets spotted by the target, the other can take over entirely.

With two people, your goal is to put a floating box around your target. This means that one person is in front of the target and one is behind. But with three people, you can also have a person across the street who is keeping an eye on things.

LAST THING

When secretly following someone, do not make the mistake of the four-year-old kid I was just playing hide-and-seek with. He believed that if *he* couldn't see me, then *I* couldn't see him.

So to hide, he just closed his eyes.

How dare that gnome challenge me with his primitive skills? I found him every time. *Yes!* (I'd high-five you right now, but it's apparently impossible.) The tyke reminded me of the people who walk around with their hoodies pulled over their heads. You just know that lots of them are categorizing the rest of the world as out of sight, out of mind.

If you're trying to conceal your identity, don't pull up your hoodie. It just makes you look *more* suspicious. And I guess that's a good reminder that it's time for me to talk about disguises!

DISGUISES, ALIBIS, AND COVERS!

When it comes to concealing your identity, nothing works better than using a rubber cow.

Don't believe me? During World War II, British agents came up with a collapsible rubber cow disguise. Just like in cartoons, it had room for one person to be the head and two front legs, and another agent would be the cow's back legs and butt. And just like in cartoons, I'm sure this led to some interesting arguments!

The idea was that two spies would parachute at night into a pasture with cows in it. Genius! The spies would conceal their parachutes and then hide in the cow outfit in case anyone came looking for them.

But even if you have a cow costume, how are you ever going to disguise yourself? You don't even know what *you* look like. Of course, neither do I! Here's what I mean: if you've listened to your voice on a recording, you might not think it sounds like you—even though it does! That's because it's hard to get a good perspective on *yourself*. You're too close to the subject.

So while you *think* you know what you look like, you really don't. And this makes disguising yourself difficult! To get around this problem, ask four people to make a short list of your most visible, obvious features. In other words, if you were standing in a crowd, what would someone notice about you? These are *not* value judgments, so don't take them personally. Also, we're not doing a fashion makeover here. We're just trying to define what fashion of person you *already* are.

Disguises, Alibis, and Covers!

Now, look at the feedback you've gotten and see what you can do to disguise yourself!

You walk funny.	Walk seriously.
You have long hair.	Buy a skullcap, hairnet, or visit the barber.
You are short.	Wear platform shoes and long pants.
You are tall.	Look, do I have to figure out *everything*?
You mope and wear a lot of black clothing.	Smile and wear Hawaiian shirts and Californian pants.
You are thin.	Wear thick padded clothing.
You are thick and padded.	Wear thin clothing.
You wear glasses.	Take the glasses off. (Good luck!)
You have a big Adam's apple.	Wear a fake neckbeard.
You are elderly.	Carry a child safety seat. (Tell people it's for you.)
You are young.	Squint and tell "the whipper-snappers" to stop muttering.

You should realize by now that spies can be *anywhere*. They are professionals at blending in. This especially applies to spy-assassins. There was a case in Dubai where 11 disguised assassins walked into a luxury hotel. And after they arrived, the spies "removed" (okay, killed) a terrorist leader. What kinds of awesome disguises did these murderous pros use? Hats, glasses, and fake beards. That's it!

PORTRAIT OF AN ASSASSIN

These items were easy for the agents to add or subtract from their disguises—and that's the key. An important part of disguising yourself is being able to make quick changes. For example, you've probably heard of reversible jackets. Let me suggest taking that idea one step further. I have two words for you: *reversible underwear*. One quick trip to the bathroom and *ta-dah*! Of course, no one else will notice the change, but you'll act differently. (Maybe.) And people will *definitely* think you're a different person if you add or remove a bad hairweave, straw hat, gold tooth, or even a cast for a broken arm.

To make quick changes, it's important to carry a change of clothes in a backpack or duffel bag. But (and this is important) have a *different* backpack or duffel bag inside of the one you're carrying. That way, when you duck into a restroom to put on an overcoat, fake goatee, and a homburg (that's a hat), you won't come out still carrying the same old Adidas bag.

NOT-SO QUICK CHANGES!

★ Grow a beard.
★ Cut your beard.
★ Let your hair grow out.
★ Cut your hair.
★ Put a scarf around your throat.
★ Cut your thro—*hey, wait a minute!*

Just as important as your appearance is your body language. If you're American, it's likely that people from other countries will notice that you put your hands in your pockets, slouch, lean against walls, and chew gum. (Seriously.) So don't do *any* of those things when you're out on a mission! Instead, try standing up straight and using your hands a lot when you talk.

It's also possible to change the way you walk. Try putting a pebble in one shoe and a slice of Swiss cheese (cheddar also works) in the other. As your feet go through strange new sensations, you will find yourself walking with a new disguised gait. Speaking of shoes, if you ever want to use your shoes as a special tool for walking in a whole different manner, put them on the wrong feet (left shoe on right foot and vice versa). Trust me, it works wonders!

As for your voice, it's possible to disguise it during phone conversations. But don't try to fake an accent! You will just sound like yourself trying to fake an accent. Instead, take a pen or pencil and put it between your teeth. Then speak carefully. This will change your speech enough to fool whoever is on the other line. And the amazing thing is—*ouch*!

DO YOU SUFFER FROM NINJAVITIS?

Sorry, I just had a sharp pain. You see, I suffer from *ninjavitis*. This is a condition where ninja assassins make frequent attempts on your life. As annoying as these murderous pests can be, ninjas can also teach us a few things about concealment. You see, the word *ninja* comes from the Japanese word *ninjitsu*—the art of making oneself invisible. Based on the movies I've watched, the first way to go about this is to wear a black coverall with a hoodie and a face mask. You may scoff, but as far as I can see, once you put on this getup, you can walk on tight-ropes and hang from trees by your toes for hours on end.

Going black has its advantages, especially at night. But when you go out in the day, go gray. That means blending in with your surroundings so that you can disappear in a crowd of two. Do most people your size and age wear T-shirts and sneakers? Then do the same thing and watch how invisible you become. On the other hand, maybe top hats and cummerbunds are the cool threads in your part of the world. If so, start packing! Because it's time to move to a place where people wear T-shirts and sneakers.

The following goes without saying, so I'll write it: If you're disguising yourself, be sure to remove anything distinctive that you usually wear, like jewelry, suspenders, or tattoos. Don't wear white shoes, and don't wear clothes that contrast with each other, like a dark shirt with a light jacket. Try to dress generically. Just try to fit in and act normally. In a library? Carry a book. In an animal feed store? Carry a pig.

We can learn a valuable lesson about concealment from King Alfred of Britain. After his kingdom was invaded by Vikings, Alfred dressed up as a minstrel (a wandering music maker) and then went to the Viking camp. Alfred was able to get into the camp and play a harp near the tent where the Viking commanders were making their plans. Talk about getting some good intelligence!

Later, when Alfred led his army into battle, not only did he win, but he also earned a cool nickname: King Alfred the Great. (That's better than his other nickname, King Alfred the Harpist.)

When spies like King Alfred go into enemy territory, they have to be extra careful. That's why British spies landing on beaches in Asia during World War II wore special boots that left behind barefoot-shaped imprints in the sand.

FOR WHEN YOU'RE SPYING ON GIBBONS

In the late 1960s, makeup master John Chambers did the costumes for the *Planet of the Apes* movie. After the movie came out, CIA officials were so impressed, they hired Chambers to do disguises for government agents!

An unusual disguise was used in the Civil War by a spy pretending to be a black male slave. The slave was actually a woman named Sarah Emma Edmonds . . . a white woman. Working for the Union, Ms. Edmonds cut her hair, wore a wig, and dyed her skin darker . . . and incredibly, the disguise worked!

If Edmonds could pull off that disguise, then it's entirely possible that you have seen a disguised agent before. You just didn't know it at the time! The agent may even have been wearing a mask—and not some cheesy Halloween-type mask either. The CIA makes the best masks in the world. They allow the skin beneath the mask to breathe and appear totally natural.

HIDING THINGS!

Whether you're at home or on the road, as a spy you're going to need to learn how to disguise and hide your secret stuff. Let's go over some tips:

1. Do *not* hide things under the bed, under the mattress, in your pillow, or in your shoes. Do you know why? Because that's where everyone always looks!

2. Some people have had success hiding valuables in the freezer. This is an especially good place to keep any ice cubes you have that are collector's items.

3. This is a really cool tip: Experts often put valuables in a large ziplock freezer bag. But they don't put the bag in the freezer. Instead, they use safety pins to fasten the bag to the *inside* of clothes that are hanging in the closet. No one would ever think to check there! This technique also works with curtains or drapes as long as the bag is pinned so that it's not visible from inside or outside.

ALIBIS AND COVERS

While having a complicated disguise is not necessary to be a spy, having an *alibi* is. Your alibi is your false reason for being where you are. The key is to have a good alibi. And make sure to have the right props and pocket litter to back up your identity. ("Pocket litter" is what spies call the stuff in your pockets that make your story real.)

For instance, "I'm here doing a survey" is a good alibi, but it's worthless if you don't have a computer tablet or a clipboard with some paper. And if you ask, "Have you seen this dog? I'm looking for her!" you should be able to show a photo of a dog—*and* you should be carrying a leash.

Oh, and be sure to give out your *cryptonym*. That's an agent's fake name.

SCOUT'S HONOR

If you're a really smooth operator, you won't even need to explain your alibi. Just look at Robert Baden-Powell. He originated the Scout movement in 1907, and founded the Boy Scouts a few years later. But he was also a British agent who loved adventure and enjoyed acting. This led to escapades like the time he once drenched his clothes in brandy and then wandered out on a military dock in Germany to spy on a ship. Baden-Powell was immediately arrested. Oops! But since he reeked of alcohol and was acting drunk, Baden-Powell was sent on his way—having gotten the information he wanted!

On a mission to Croatia in the late 1800s, Baden-Powell's job was to learn about the strength of the forts in the region. So he took a sketchbook and a butterfly net and set out. Baden-Powell then disguised his sketches of fort layouts within his sketches of butterfly wings.

POWERPOINT

You can easily do something similar on a computer. Just take your secret document or information. Now select all the text and copy it into a PowerPoint document. Select and change the color of the text so that it matches the background. And now, copy and paste a big picture over the whole thing. When you send it to another agent, all that person has to do is delete the picture and then highlight the text behind it to reveal your message!

COVER: A FALSE IDENTITY

While a cryptonym can conceal your name, you might need to conceal your *identity*. That means you need something stronger than an alibi—you need a *cover*. A cover is your false identity or job. It's the same thing as an alibi but just more complicated.

Picking the right cover is important! It has to be something that you can fake doing reasonably well. For example, Rita Elliott was a Russian spy. Her cover? Well, she worked in a circus. Good cover! This gave Rita a chance to travel all over without looking suspicious. But Rita's job at the circus was as a tightrope walker. This could be a very bad cover if she hadn't been skilled at her work.

ANIMAL SPIES!

As we know, the key for any spy is not to look suspicious. And what's less suspicious than an animal? Well, okay, a *plant* is less suspicious, but it's really hard to get a birch tree or even a small shrub to follow orders. And that's why critters, beasts, and varmints have been used many, many times in the world of espionage.

What—you think animals haven't won or lost wars before? Ha! About 2,500 years ago, spies from Persia noted that their Egyptian rivals loved cats. So when Persia went to war with Egypt in 525 BCE, the Persians had a secret weapon: as the Persian soldiers marched forward, they held kitty cats.

Since the Egyptians thought cats were the coolest animals of all time, they wouldn't shoot any arrows at the

Persians. And it was hard to win a battle back then without shooting arrows. So the Egyptians lost!

This shows that the Egyptians were wrong about two things: how to win a war and what the coolest animal of all time is. You see, the Egyptians *should* have focused their attention on . . .

DOGS!

Almost all people like and trust dogs. That's why they can be the ideal helpers for a spy! For example, a French agent used a dog as an assistant during World War II. The agent was in a part of Southeast Asia that was under

Japanese control. The agent knew that if he were caught sending a secret message to the French, it would mean certain death.

So he shaved his dog!

Then the spy took a pen loaded with permanent ink and wrote an intelligence report on the dog's skin. After that, all he had to do was wait for the dog's hair to grow back. As soon as Fido was hairy again, the agent just took the dog for a *long* walk and presented the canine to a French spymaster. One shave-job later and—voilà—secret message received! This message is now famous as the Dog Skin Report.[1]

THE WISDOM OF THE ANCIENTS

The Dog Skin Report was hardly the first time that tactic has been used. Back in the fifth century BCE, the Greek ruler Histiaeus devised the technique. He shaved the head of one of his servants, tattooed a message on his head, and waited for the man's hair to grow back. Then the messenger was sent on his way.

When the courier arrived at his destination, his head was shaved again and the message was read, giving information about upcoming Persian attacks. (It was Not Very Instant Messaging!)

---

1. Really. The original idea for it goes back to the ancient Greeks.

Not only can Spot carry spy messages, he can also spot spies! For instance, in 1985, the Russians suspected that their own spy, Oleg Gordievsky, was a double agent for the British. (That's because Gordievsky *was* a double agent for the British.)

Knowing he was being watched, Gordievsky left his Moscow apartment to go out for a jog—and kept on running! By bus and train, Gordievsky made it almost to Russia's border with Finland. There, he hid in the trunk of a car being driven by a female British diplomat. The woman drove up to the border, showed the KGB her papers, and got ready to drive through—until a Russian guard dog began sniffing her car's trunk. That darned dog was going to ruin Gordievsky's escape!

Thinking quickly, the woman distracted the dog with a meat sandwich. And her incredible plan worked! This led to one of the most famous rules in the history of spying: "A guard dog would rather eat baloney than sniff Gordievsky."

Speaking of dog smells, one of the strangest products the CIA ever made was a liquid that would attract male dogs and make them howl. The idea was to spray the liquid (called Dogs in Heat) on the doorsteps of suspected enemy spies at night. That way, howling dogs would annoy the agents, and they wouldn't get a good night's sleep.

LET SPYING DOGS LIE!

If you'd like to enlist your dog to confuse enemy agents, try this: Get a pair of small walkie-talkies. Using Velcro strips, attach one of them to your dog's collar. Turn on the walkie-talkie and tie a handkerchief around the dog's neck to conceal it.

Have a fellow agent take the other walkie-talkie. This agent needs to stay nearby. Now, as you walk your dog, approach enemy agents. If no enemy agents are around, just go up to anybody who doesn't seem too scary. Act casual when your dog makes a statement like, "We will break up your spy network and destroy you."

This might lead to the agents being tired and forgetful the next day. Maybe they would do something dumb, like leave their secret documents at the ice cream shop. (Hey, you never know!)

Because spies love disguises, sometimes *they* like to be the dog. Seriously! In the 1970s, the CIA came up with a way for an agent to sneak around in a country without being detected. First, one agent would enter the country with a Saint Bernard dog. These colossal hounds can be the size of a small pony!

Then if another spy needed to get somewhere unobserved, he would check in with the Saint Bernard's owner. There, the spy would put on a Saint Bernard dog suit and crawl into a portable kennel. The spy would also bring a small tape player and begin playing the sounds a Saint Bernard makes: snoring, slobbering, and snoring.

The kennel would then be transported to a veterinarian so the "dog" could get a checkup. Once inside the vet's office, the spy would get out of the kennel, take off the dog suit, and leave. But he probably wouldn't bring the tape of snoring and slobbering, as it's unlikely that it would be helpful with his assignment.

If anyone was observing all this, all they saw was that the "dog" was left overnight at the vet's for observation.

WHEN HAMSTERS INFILTRATE YOUR HOME

If you have a hamster cage or aquarium in your house, try this spy trick. See if there's a spot where you can place or mount a cell phone behind the cage or aquarium. The idea is that you're going to take a photo (or series of photos) from that spot, using the camera's timer. And because the photo will show the room seemingly from inside the animals' habitat, it will look like the hamster or guppy took the picture!

Assuming you have your phone ready and the timer set, simply wait until you hear people coming into the room. Then set the camera and stand back so you don't block the shot. Be sure to have the flash turned off and the camera sound on mute. If you can only take one shot at a time with your automatic settings, you might have to do this a few times to get the shots you want, but patience is an important part of spy work. (If you're not that patient, just use the phone's video instead.)

Once you have your shots, print them out and put them in a manila envelope. Then write a note, maybe something along the lines of "I've been spying on you for months. If you don't want me to tell the authorities about you, start giving me better hamster (or guppy) chow. And plenty of it!"

Shove the envelope through your mail slot (or use the hamster's e-mail address and send the photos to your victim as attachments), and try to keep a straight face.

SEA LIONS AND DOLPHINS!

The elite US Navy unit named SEALs (sea, air, and land team) is made up of humans. But the navy also has a Marine Mammal Program in San Diego that trains California sea lions and bottlenose dolphins. I love dolphins—they're so cute! But what could these delightful mammals be doing for the military?

Apparently, the dolphins can go get enemy divers! One navy animal trainer said, "We train them to either pull the mouthpiece from the diver's mouth or push him to the surface." Apparently, dolphins have been armed with syringes loaded with pressurized gas. And if this syringe were poked into a human diver, it would cause the person to blow up. *Blech!*

I guess dolphins aren't so cute anymore.

Along with sea lions, dolphins are both very intelligent and *way* faster in the water than even the best human swimmers. Navy sea lions are trained to carry cuffs in their mouths that are attached to long ropes. If they find a suspicious swimmer, they can clamp the cuff around the person's leg and the intruder is then reeled in like a big spy fish.

And it turns out that even the most skilled divers usually never even see the sea lion before being clamped and hauled to the surface.

And the sea lion will do all this for some *fish*! Amazing.

Current plans are for dolphins to patrol the waters off US bases to watch out for terrorist swimmers. If the dolphin on patrol sees an intruder, it activates a powerful strobe light to alert its handlers. The light would then float to the surface, and guards would race there in speedboats.

A trained marine mammal can also locate and retrieve lost objects, or look for underwater mines. (Seriously, the animals are trained to do that.)

But what if a sea lion or dolphin accidentally triggers the mine and gets blown up? Sad! So to prevent that, the US Navy developed underwater robots that check for mines instead.

Called unmanned underwater vehicles (UUVs), four of these water robots were put to the test by the navy. Oops! All four of the UUVs were lost at sea. So who did the navy send to find them? The same dolphins and sea lions the robots were supposed to replace!

CATS!

As I noted earlier, cats can be useful. After all, cats are known and loved for their intelligence and grace. And they're also known for their cunning, paranoia, and murderous impulses.

Wait a minute, cats are *totally* untrustworthy!

No matter. Back in the 1960s, the CIA recruited cats to be part of their spy program. The felines were going to take part in Operation Acoustic Kitty. (No, I am not making this up.) The idea was that a cat would be trained to follow certain commands. Then it would be outfitted with a little microphone and antenna. When ready, the cat would slink around during a cocktail party and listen in on people's top secret discussions about nuclear missiles and cheese-on-a-toothpick.

Perhaps you can see the problem with Operation Acoustic Kitty. Yep, it's the "cat would be trained" part! It turns out that in the history of mankind, no cat has ever been trained to do *anything*. So if the acoustic kitty was released at a party, it was totally unreliable. The program ended when a CIA agent released a spy cat in a park to go eavesdrop on some people. The cat ignored orders and strolled off into the street, where it was hit by a car!

That was the end of Operation Acoustic Kitty.

VOCABULARY

Walking the cat is what CIA agents do when an operation goes wrong. The idea is to go back to its beginning, and then walk through the plan again to spot where it went off target.

PARACHUTING BEARS?

Could parachute-wearing bears sniff out a terrorist? I mean, a bear's sense of smell is much more powerful than a bloodhound's. So why not use bears to sniff out bad guys?

The Defense Department gets suggestions from the public all the time. Sometimes citizens write in with good ideas. Sometimes the ideas are decent. And sometimes the ideas are insane.

Take this idea about terrorist-hunting bears. Before the terrorist Osama bin Laden was killed in 2011, this suggestion was sent to the Defense Department: "Trained bears with GPS and cameras around their necks might be able to hunt down the scent of Osama bin Laden, even in and through any caves and tunnels! Parachute some bears into areas [that bin Laden] might be. Attempt to train [the] bears to take off parachutes after landing, or use parachutes that self-destruct after landing."

Well, that sounds simple enough! Ooh, and here's a different citizen question for the Defense Department:

"So do you have any top secret information you would like to tell me? I am doing a project for my senior economics class, and was just wondering . . . e-mail me back."

BIRDS!

Back in the primitive days of the twentieth century, there were no cell phones. (Astounding!) So animals were sometimes used to carry important messages. And that's why British and American forces used hundreds of thousands of messenger pigeons in both World Wars I and II. This could be dangerous for the birds. Once, when an American battalion began getting shelled by their own forces miles away, they used a pigeon to take word back to the nimrods shooting at them to lay off.

The pigeon was named Cher Ami. And that brave little

pigeon got his message through despite losing an eye
and a leg on the flight.

Cher Ami was treated like a hero after his mission, but
not all of our feathered agents are so lucky. For example,
a pigeon in India was once captured and held under
armed guard. Why? It was suspected of being a spy for
India's archenemy, Pakistan!

Indians grew suspicious when they spotted a pigeon
with a ring around its foot. And once it was captured,
Indian pigeon keepers insisted that the bird was totally
suspicious. This was partly because of the Pakistani
phone number and address stamped on its body in red
ink—and also because the experts said that Pakistani

pigeons look totally different from Indian ones!

Sadly, the pigeon couldn't tell its story. After all, you can't expect a pigeon to sing like a canary. But if the pigeon is a foreign agent, it's not going to be returned. This means that Pakistan gave India the bird![2]

WORMS!

You probably already know that silk comes from silkworms. (These are actually moth caterpillars, but whatever.) And these silkworms spin silk out of their butts! That's a pretty good trick. I'd like to see a sheep try that with wool! (Actually, I wouldn't.)

Until fairly recently in human history, most of the world didn't know what silk was, much less where it came from. But then about 1,500 years ago, the ruler of the Byzantine Empire (in southeastern Europe and Turkey) sent spies to China with hollow walking sticks. Their mission was to pretend to be messengers looking for a trade agreement. Actually, they were supposed to be finding and stashing silk moth eggs in their walking sticks to smuggle home!

Silkworms aren't even the only worms involved in espionage. During World War I, British spies faced a problem: How could they read maps at night without

---

2. Did you see that? Two jokes in one little paragraph!

attracting enemy fire? The solution was to read by the light of glowworms! Sure, the Brits had to strain their eyes by the glowworms' pale light, but that still beats getting a howitzer shell up the nose.

SNEAKING, FOLLOWING, AND ESCAPING!

I got in trouble the first time I went out on a mission. It was just myself and an agent named [name deleted]. As the two of us made dead drops, staked out enemy agents, and stopped for a quick shopping trip (I had a coupon for pickles!), I'd tweet our precise location. (I did this so my mother would know that her favorite child was safe.)

But when [name deleted] found out what I was doing, she was *not* amused. She took away my iPhone, deleted my Twitter account, and confiscated my pickle jar.

Luckily, I had another coupon!

Anyway, my theory now is that spies should be like hikers. That's because when hikers go into the wilderness, their goal is to *leave no trace* that they were there. Nothing but bootprints—and maybe some buried poop. As a spy, you want to follow that example! (Except for the part about the poop.)

So develop your powers of observation and cunning! Let's say that you've been tipped off about a top secret item that's in a room. Don't just go waltzing in to take it. Waltzing is always suspicious! As you approach the room's door, carefully look at the handle *before* opening it. Why? It's possible that someone has sprinkled a small amount of baby powder on the handle to see if any intruders tried to enter.

The KGB invented a "spy dust" that could be revealed using infrared lights. It was sprinkled on the doorknobs to important rooms. Then guards or officers would shine infrared lights on people's hands to see if anyone had been sneaking around.

It's also common for paranoid people (like me!) to place a small piece of clear tape on the door and frame. That way, if an agent returns to a room and the door tape is broken, she knows someone has been in there.

SOLUTION: Avoid touching the handle's powder or sprinkle new powder on it as you exit. As for the tape, open the door. But when you leave the room, replace the tape with a new piece.[1]

If the door is unlocked, you can enter the room safely. But when you push the handle down or turn the knob, *keep* it pushed down or turned until you're through the door. Then gently close it and slowly let the handle of the knob latch. Nice and quiet.

If the door is locked, just use a key. No key? Pick the lock, already! (You'll find lock-picking instructions on page 783 of this book.) As you're walking in, you feel the small rug in front of the door give way slightly beneath your feet. Aha!

Rolling up strips of modeling clay and putting them under a rug is yet another way of seeing if an intruder has come into a room. If you return and find that the strips of clay have been squished, it's a giveaway.

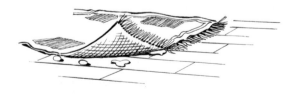

---

1. Instead of using tape, some people wet a long hair and stick it to the doorframe. Disgusting! So if you see a hairy door, avoid it.

SOLUTION: When you leave, carefully lift the rug, reroll any clay strips you might have squished, and step around the rug on your way out.

Finally you approach the desk. You can see that what you're looking for is underneath a tray of marbles. Why marbles? Because whoever set up the tray took a photo of exactly where the marbles are!

SOLUTION: Take a photo of the marbles. After getting what you came for, rearrange the marbles according to the photo.

Now you're almost there. After moving the tray to the side, you're ready to accomplish your act of espionage. It looks like that box of Cap'n Crunch is waiting for you! Uh-oh . . . you need a bowl and some milk!

SOLUTION: Get a bowl and some milk.

In the event that you found like a secret file, you need to get it and get out. But the problem with going out the door you came in is that you can't see through it! What if a big security guard is approaching from the other side? To detect the presence of approaching meanies, lean down and gently place your front teeth on the door handle. The best way to detect vibrations is to touch metal, and few things are as sensitive to vibrations as your teeth! Is it silly for a spy to seemingly be eating a door handle? Yes. Does this work? Yes!

SNEAKING QUIETLY

So let's say that you're trying to move around without making a sound. Yes, that rhymes, but that's not important now. What is important is that you're not carrying any keys. They jingle! And turn off your cell phone, too.

For maximum silence, don't wear wooden clogs, and avoid corduroy clothing because the fabric rubs against itself. Some spies think wool is the quietest fabric. But other spies think *no* fabric is the quietest fabric of all. For them, the best disguise is no disguise . . . and no clothing, either!

Before doing any professional sneaking, you may want to practice sneaking up on animals. That's because an animal has senses that are far more sensitive than a human. So, if you can sneak up on a cat, you can *definitely* sneak up on an enemy agent.

I'm practicing this right now with our tomcat, Captain Sugarmittens. Ha! This furball is sleeping so deeply, he doesn't realize that I'm reaching out right now to grab his tail—

Aaah, get him off my face!!!!

Oh, you are bad, Captain Sugarmittens. You just gave

your daddy a third nostril! But at least I learned a valuable lesson. When indoors, you can avoid making floorboards and old stairs creak by stepping as close to the wall as possible. That's how Captain Sugarmittens caught me just now.

So *that's* the reason why spies and cats both skulk! I mean, have you ever seen a cat go through a doorway? It stays close to the edge of the door and peers around the corner with one eye. If the coast is clear, the cat goes through but still sticks by the wall.

Cats also like to stay close to things they can hide behind, like sofas, chairs, and larger, fatter cats. Since these cats need the exercise, let's go *outside* for the rest of this training. Now, if you ever find yourself sneaking around in woods like these, try to avoid stepping on the dry twigs—

crunch

Who was that? Mom? Timmy?

crunch

Captain Sugarmittens?

Wait, it's me! And if I'm trying to creep up on someone, I still haven't given myself away yet. With dry forest floors, don't just plod along with a *crunch, crunch, crunch*. Instead, try to take irregular steps. That means you might *crunch, crunch* [pause, slide your foot, stop for 20 seconds] *crunch*, etc. There are all sorts of animals out in the forest, and you might be able to fool someone listening into thinking that you're one of them.

BEING TAILED

Do you think you're being followed? Maybe you are! If you've noticed someone near you twice in one day, it could just be a coincidence. But if you're out and about, and you see your suspect 17 times, that's too coincidental to be a coincidence! You're under surveillance! Try these tactics:

1. If you constantly look back, your tail will know that she's been spotted. So if you're on foot in a city, glance at shop windows to look behind you. Pop into a store, glance at a rack of bibs, and then pop back out. This gives you a chance to survey the whole street in both directions before setting off again.

2. Try turning a corner and quickly putting on or taking off a hat or jacket. Or turn a corner and run fast for a few steps. Or turn a corner and duck into a shop or doorway.

3. I guess what I'm saying here is that you need to turn a corner.

4. If you spot the person who you think is following you, turn around sharply and start walking in the opposite direction. As soon as your tail's back is

to you, start running! Then turn around and see what your suspect is doing. (Note: be careful, as you're now sprinting in one direction and looking in another.)

5. The *best* way to spot a tail is to have a team (or at least one other person) working with you. The idea is that your team tails you while looking for anyone else who looks like they're tailing you too. You can station members of your team at certain choke points where flow is restricted. These choke points might be narrow sidewalks, entrances or exits, or spots where people are choking on food that they should have chewed more before trying to swallow.

VOCABULARY

Dry cleaning: The process of using a team to spot a tail.

Here's something you already know: People who get on escalators face in the direction they're traveling . . . and almost never turn around! So if you get on an escalator, go about halfway up and then quickly turn around. Did someone behind you quickly look away? They're busted! And if a team of people is trailing you, there is probably someone in *front* of you as well. Watch the people getting off; does anyone turn to check if you're there or loiter at the top of the escalator? If so, they're busted, too!

EXIT ROUTES

As you've been learning, making a getaway requires advance planning. So imagine you're at home lounging in your pajamas and enjoying educational cartoons. Then suddenly, you see enemy agents closing in!

This is when your organization pays off. You sprint toward the TV, open the bottom cabinet doors, and access the escape tunnel you put in months ago.

Or perhaps you're spending quality time at the playground. From atop the slide, you spot a group of enemy parents pushing their heavily armed strollers closer! You quickly slide down the slide and run to the swings!

Getting a nearby kid to push you, you soar through the air, and leap into the sandbox. From there, you access the escape tunnel you put in months ago. Crawling through it, you finally emerge through its trapdoor, which happens to be right back at the . . . slide.

Uh-oh.

TRAVEL TIPS

When staying at a hotel, stay away from the ground floor. That makes it too easy for enemy agents to sneak into your room. It will also make it harder for them to throw things like stun grenades or fattening snacks through your window.

Speaking of which, have you ever been in a hotel room that had a shared balcony with the room next door? For obvious reasons, you don't want that kind of room. Also, avoid any room that is across from another room with higher windows. (This makes it too easy to spy on you!)

Okay, so now you're headed to your room. A bellhop stops you in the hallway and asks what room number you're in. What do you do? If you've been paying attention, you give him a *fake* room number. That punk could be a spy! After all, bellhops are naturally suspicious . . . what job could possibly involve *bells* and *jumping*?

Continuing, you take the elevator to the floor *above* your actual floor. Then you take the stairs down. Why? A spy never goes right to his destination.

As you get settled in, you check your luggage for the doorstop you packed. These little wedges are handy to insert beneath the door when you're in a room. That way, even if someone has a key to your room, they can't get in!

Okay, you're safe and sound—wait, you left your fattening snacks in the lobby? Dang it!

ASSASSINATION!

Look, I'm not writing about antisocial topics like assassination because I'm antisocial. I'm *very* social. I even go out of my way to have tea and crumpets with little old ladies.

Wait, what *is* a crumpet, anyway? Dang, my own misinformation just tripped me up!

Maybe a crumpet is kind of like a pancake. Which reminds me: During World War II, American scientists came up with an explosive that looked like wheat flour and could be used to make pancakes. The pancakes were even edible. But if you attached a detonator, they'd explode. Those pancakes were dynamite!

So they were an excellent tool for an *assassination* at breakfast. Assassination is the murder of a usually important person in a surprise attack for political reasons. But I'm so nonviolent, I know I could never stab someone—heck, I can't even jab those sharp straws into a juice box. So when it comes to assassination, exploding pancakes sound pretty good to me.

When a spy gets what's called a wet job, that means it is a mission that might involve people bleeding. So if you're assigned to a wet job, dress appropriately. For example, bloodstains don't show up as well on dark clothing. And waterproof fabrics won't stain at all!

But then there is the *wrong* kind of a wet job. Did you know that when world leaders visit the United States, they pee and poop? It's true! And if someone were to collect some of the pee and poop, *that* would be intelligence! By analyzing a person's number two, you can find

CHEMICAL AGENTS

Cleisthenes of Sicyon was an ancient Greek leader who liked to conquer other cities. But at least the headman did it in creative ways. To take over one town, Cleisthenes had his agents put a powerful laxative in its water. As the poor townspeople ran around, desperately looking for a place to poop, Cleisthenes' soldiers waltzed in and took over.

out what their health is like. So, when possible, that's exactly what intelligence agents doo-doo.

Ooh, here's a *really* wet job. In 1950, an American agent named Edward Lansdale was in the Philippines working against a Communist group. Knowing that there were local superstitions about vampires, Lansdale spread rumors that bloodsuckers were out and about.

After Lansdale's Filipino allies killed a Communist in battle, the American would have the dead man's throat punctured and his blood drained. And when the Communist's body was later found, this would spook everyone . . . especially the Communists!

Anyway, now that you've read this far, someone (maybe a family member!) may try to hire you to assassinate one of their enemies. When this happens, remember to stay cool.

Assassination!

YOUR UNCLE (whispering): I hear you know where the bodies are buried.
YOU (blowing a bubble with your bubblegum): And I know how to add more!

You may be tempted to accept an assassination job, but there are very good reasons to say no. First, the word "ass" is in "assassination" *twice*. This may be a sign that you should *think* twice about taking these jobs.

More importantly, killing people is not only illegal but also dangerous. You see, people who engage in treacherous violence often become *victims* of treacherous violence!

For example, Russians once hired two men to assassinate a German diplomat. The assassins were each given a camera case. One camera case was red and one was blue. The assassins were told to press a button on the *red* case, which would activate a bomb inside of it.

After the explosion, they were to push a button on the *blue* case, which would lay down a smoke screen and allow them to escape.

But the assassins were suspicious. Since when is a smoke screen *that* important for a getaway? Plus, secondhand smoke-screen smoke is bad for you! So as an experiment, the agents pressed the button on the *blue* camera case. Bad move! It turned out that this case *also* contained a bomb, and both men were blown up!

(Boy, you just can't trust anyone.)

The word "assassin" comes from a group of Muslims who lived in Iran a thousand years ago. Led by Hassan-e Sabbah, these Muslims sent trained killers to stab any leader who took hostile action against them.

Today, many believe that the killers sent out on these death missions became known as "followers of Hassan," or Assassins. These Assassins sometimes spent years stalking their victims before finally choosing the moment of truth. So the killer needed to be able to infiltrate an enemy community with a good cover story. And when the Assassin chose his moment, he would try to stab his victim in the most *public* place possible. The more crowds and the more guards, the better! This would terrify people and give the Assassins a psychological edge.

Of course, after stabbing their targets, Assassins were usually killed by bodyguards. And because of that, some historians point to the Assassins as the world's first terrorists. But that's not quite fair. The Assassins targeted leaders who had *already* attacked their group. The idea of killing innocent unarmed people (like modern terrorists do) would have been revolting to them.

Hey, maybe the Assassins *saved* lives! By killing hostile leaders, the Assassins prevented wars that would have killed far more people than *one*. And it's not like the Assassins stabbed everybody who bothered them. For instance, Hassan-e Sabbah was once concerned about a sultan who was ordering military expeditions against the Assassins.

So one morning, the sultan woke up in his bedchamber and found a dagger plunged into the floor next to his bed!

Later that day, the sultan got a message from the Assassins: "Did I not wish the sultan well, that dagger which was stuck into the hard ground would have been planted in his soft chest."

Hassan didn't have any trouble from the sultan after that!

The Assassins left us the word *assassin*, and also the knowledge that even the best bodyguards can't stop a killer from getting to a leader. Because of that, there is an unspoken rule in the world today that no leader of a nation (especially a democracy) should order the assassination of another leader. Because once someone does

CLOAKS AND DAGGERS

The traditional symbols for spies are the cloak and the dagger. The cloak is handy for hiding things like the spy himself, as well as the dagger he is holding. The dagger is handy for assassinations and can also be used to spread butter on toast.

that, then *anyone* could be fair game and *no one* would be safe!

But there was one national leader who was the exception to this rule—Fidel Castro (1926–2016), the president of Cuba.

FIDEL CASTRO: THE CIA REALLY HATED THAT GUY!

From the moment Castro became president in 1959, he inspired the weirdest assassination attempts you can imagine. For example, since the Cuban leader loved to smoke cigars, CIA agents got the not-very-great idea to use cigars to kill him! The agents came up with two plans:

1. In 1961, a Cuban double agent was given a cigar that had been poisoned. The spy was to give Castro the cigar, and after the Cuban leader smoked it, he'd be dead. But either Castro never smoked the cigar, or there wasn't enough poison in it.

2. An exploding cigar was made to give Castro. According to an agent, the cigar was so powerful, it would "blow his head off"! But again, he never smoked it.

After their cigar ideas fizzled, CIA agents tried other ideas to assassinate Castro. (Boy, they really hated that guy!) These other attempts included a poisoned scuba-diving suit, an exploding seashell, and enlisting Mafia hit men.

These plans all failed. So in 1963, the all-time most insane concept was invented: a poison pen! Here's how it worked: Castro would pick up the pen and push down on the pen's button to get the ballpoint end to come out. When he did this, a small needle would stick out of the button, poisoning him. Then the Cuban dictator would finally die, die, *die*!

So did it work? Ha! Over 50 years after the poison pen idea, Castro died in 2016 at the age of 90.

DEADLY WEAPONS

Ouch! Sorry, I'm nursing an injury right now. I was spying at a croquet tournament, and one of the balls caught me *right* on the ankle. Dang, those things are hard! It's like they're made of wood or something. In fact, it's clear to me that a croquet ball (or the mallet used to hit it) could be used as a death-dealing weapon of deadliness!

But do you know the *most* deadly weapon that people use daily? The *car*. That's right. Each day, billions of people get behind the steering wheel and zoom down the street inside of several tons of hard steel. Get in their way and you'll be crushed.

This is not to suggest that you learn how to drive so

you can destroy enemy agents. But be aware that *they* might be out there gunning the engine for you! And these automotive assassins don't need to be in a minivan to do you in. For instance, here are three nonmotorized vehicles your assassin could choose instead:

Bicycle

DANGER: It's faster than you.

GOOD DEFENSE: Run behind a tree.

BAD DEFENSE: Run down the middle of the street.

FUN FACT: If the assassin runs you down, he will probably wipe out.

Skateboard

DANGER: Skateboarders have no fear. (Their T-shirts even say so!)

GOOD DEFENSE: Run by a skate ramp. (Skateboarders are easily distracted.)

BAD DEFENSE: Stand at the bottom of the skate ramp.

FUN FACT: Even if you get hit, you're safe from the ankles up!

Tricycle

DANGER: Three wheels = three nasty rubber marks as they roll over you.

GOOD DEFENSE: Avoid spots where trikers hang out, like playgrounds and triker bars.

BAD DEFENSE: Getting on a tricycle to escape. (You're too big!)

FUN FACT: Alexander the Great never used tricycles when he conquered the world.

To be prepared when a desperado confronts you with murder in his eyes and wax in his ears, know these three simple rules:

1. WEAPONS ARE *EVERYWHERE*. A weapon doesn't have to be a knife or a tricycle. A banana is a weapon. True, it doesn't stab very well, and bananas rarely explode. But what if someone was chasing you and slipped on a banana peel that you had put there? I have heard of things like this happening. (Of course, I also watch a lot of cartoons.)

   However, your opponents may use something more sophisticated than a banana. For instance, DARPA (see page 50) is working on scopes for rifles that will enable snipers to shoot targets from almost two miles away—in heavy winds. And the snipers may be using bullets that can change course in midair. (Seriously.) If your enemies have one of these, you'd better have a pretty high-tech banana to protect yourself. (Or maybe a mango!)

2. REACT, DON'T DRAW! In the event that you find yourself having to draw a weapon against an enemy agent,

let *her* make the first move. Studies suggest that you will draw 10 percent faster if you're reacting than if you draw your own gun first. And that 10 percent should make up for your opponent's advantage. Unless it doesn't!

3. USE SURPRISE TO YOUR ADVANTAGE. For instance, what if a ninja sprang out of your closet right now? Admittedly, if you're not reading this book in your bedroom, it wouldn't make much of an impression. And if you *were* home, it would be suicidal to engage in hand-to-hand combat with the ninja. That's because it's foolish to only fight with *one* hand. Next time, try *hands-to-hands* combat.

Running away is not very dignified behavior for an intelligence agent, plus you might get a ninja star thrown at your butt.

So as the ninja advances, quickly look around you for weapons. You see a laptop, some computer cords, a number of pens and pencils, a small waste-paper basket, and an electric fan. So what do you do that would surprise the ninja?

Turn the fan on high, rip off its protective cover, and chop that ninja up with its soft, rubber blades. Then dispose of the ninja pieces in the wastebasket.

Or you could hit Save on your document and shut down your laptop properly. After that's done, detach the computer's power cable and use it as a strangling device called a *garrote* (guh-ROTE).

GARROTE DEFENSE!

A garrote is a wire used to strangle someone. Assassins like to use garrotes because they're silent killers. The idea is that the agent approaches someone like a guard from behind and loops a wire around their neck. The agent then pulls tight until the victim stops guarding and starts dying.

If you see a garrote wire suddenly looping in front of your face, pay attention! If the garrote is made with a guitar string, it's a good bet that your wannabe assassin plays guitar. Lunge for a drum set and try to tap out a beat, however feeble. Your assassin will then release you! Why? Because no guitarist—not even a killer guitarist—can resist the temptation to jam with another musician.

On the other hand, if you're being strangled with a piano wire, you're doomed—because nobody loves playing solo more than a pianist. (Those selfish, selfish pianists!)

The best defense? If someone walks up behind you, they may cast a shadow. This gives you a chance to disarm them. (Using this method, I just disarmed a waiter of a diet soda while waiting for my lunch.)

If it seems like I'm making this sound too easy, I'm not! It turns out that lots of ninjas are dorky. For example, a group of ninjas once tried to kill General Oda Nobunaga by shooting a cannon at him. And the general was *right* in front of the cannon. They couldn't miss!

The ninjas missed.

This was because the ninja's usual job was *spying* and *sneaking* around in disguise, not killing people. And the disguises the real ninjas wore were *not* black pajamas. That would be sort of a giveaway! Instead, ninjas wore farmer outfits or the uniforms of the enemy army. One successful ninja assassination occurred when the ninja dressed as a young girl.

The legend of the black pajamas began in the 1600s. Real ninjas were disappearing as the need for spies in Japan diminished. At the same time, stories about ninjas became popular. The Japanese had a popular live theater called Kabuki. In it, puppets acted out dramas while puppet masters dressed in black outfits stood behind them. Since there was already a Japanese tradition of pretending that people in black were invisible, black became the color of choice in the new plays about fictional ninja assassins.

Assassination!

So what I'm saying is that the only ninjas to wear black pajamas have been actors!

FAKE NINJA
PAJAMAS

REAL NINJA
PAJAMAS

But if you're looking for a ninja making a real fashion statement, you should learn about the *kunoichi*. These were female ninja agents. In addition to the usual ninja skills, they were also trained to be servants or entertainers. In these roles, the kunoichi could get into an enemy camp and then gather intelligence, poison the soup, and throw *shuriken* ("sword hidden in the hand") at anybody who annoyed them!

Plus, imagine this situation. A Japanese warlord comes

upon a young woman holding a fan up to her face and weeping on the side of the road. Since men are usually more suspicious of *men*, the warlord pauses to see what's wrong.

"What's wrong?" he asks while leaning off his horse.

With a lightning-like flip, the woman flips the fan, cuts off the warlord's head, and disappears in the confusion that follows. She was a *kunoichi* with a razor-sharp fan! And her plan was totally simple, which shows what a pro she was. Because as you know, the cleverer an assassin tries to be, the more likely something will go wrong.

For example, let's say you come up with a spray gun that shoots a poisonous cyanide gas. Brilliant! There won't be any shell casings for the police to use as clues. (That's why notorious Russian agent Bogdan Stashinsky used this method.) However, this could lead to a problem:

ASSASSIN (muttering): I'll aim the poison spray gun at my victim, and *voilà*!
UNSUSPECTING VICTIM: Hmm, the wind has shifted directions!
ASSASSIN: Can't . . . breathe—*Urk*!

Clearly, assassins are sometimes just too clever for their own good. For example, in 1960, the CIA prepared a tube of poison toothpaste. It was to be slipped into the bathroom of the prime minister of the Congo. The CIA chief in the Congo vetoed the plan, but still—death by toothpaste? What next, razor-sharp dental floss?

A WEIRD PLAN THAT WORKED

North Korea has a history of assassinating people seen as threats to its government. And North Korean dictator Kim Jong-un is known to be especially ruthless. So after his older brother, Kim Jong-nam, spoke out against his family's control of the government, people worried for him.

In 2017, Kim Jong-nam was at an airport in Malaysia when two women came up behind him. The women rubbed some sort of liquid onto Kim's head and face, then ran and washed their hands. (They were arrested later.)

As for Kim, he died within just a few minutes. Even though the women didn't have guns, knives, or garrotes, they had rubbed a powerful toxic nerve agent into his skin! And although North Korea denied responsibility for the attack, nobody really bought that.

"IT'S FOR YOU."

Some villains are so mean, their assassination seems only fair. This may be true in the case of Yahya Ayyash. As the main bomb builder for a Middle East terrorist group,

Ayyash was responsible for the deaths of over 100 innocent Israeli civilians. (His skill with explosives earned him
the nickname the "Engineer.")

To rid themselves of the Engineer, Israeli agents came
up with a plan. In 1996, they made a bugged cell phone
that was also loaded with explosives. The agents then
tricked a friend of Ayyash's into giving him the phone.
And since the phone's bug revealed when the terrorist
was speaking into it, the Israeli agents knew when to activate. And they did.

THE WHITE DEATH

In 2010, the CIA fired a drone missile the size of a violin
at a terrorist in Pakistan. The missile was directed by US
agents outside of the country as it successfully hit its
target. This changed the world of assassination forever.
After all, now an assassin could be located on a different
continent than his quarry!

I wonder what Simo Häyhä would make of that. He
was a farmer living in Finland when Russia invaded his
country in 1939. To defend his homeland, Häyhä became
a sniper. Dressed in white to blend in with the Finnish
winter, Häyhä went off into the woods and started
picking off enemy soldiers. And despite the fact that he
was only about five feet tall, Häyhä soon became the

greatest sniper in history! Not only was he an amazing shot, but he had a number of tricks for staying hidden from the enemy. For instance, Häyhä held snow in his mouth while in the field, so that when he was breathing, the steam of his breath would not give away his location.

In just over three months, Häyhä shot and killed between 700 and 800 Russian soldiers. The Russians were terrified! They nicknamed Häyhä the "White Death" and sent special squads out to kill him. Those *idiots*. You

can't kill the White Death! So, the anti-Häyhä squads never returned. Can you guess why?[1]

Finally, Häyhä caught a Russian bullet in the head. The timing of this was odd because he was shot the same day that peace was declared between Finland and Russia. Anyway, Häyhä shouldn't have survived his wound. After all, when he was found, he was missing the entire left side of his face. But that's nothing to the White Death! Häyhä was nursed back to health, and he lived to be 96 years old.

THE ASSASSIN WITH A HEART

Let's end with a feel-good story. Nikolai Khokhlov was a trained Russian assassin who was assigned to kill Georgi Okolovich, a man living in Germany.

Khokhlov was armed for the job with an unusual gun: it was electrically operated, made no more noise than the snap of your fingers, fit inside a cigarette case, and fired poison-tipped bullets that might lead a coroner to think the victim had died of heart failure.

I told you this was a feel-good story!

In 1954, the Russian assassin knocked on Okolovich's apartment door. There, Khokhlov confessed that he had been sent to murder him—but his wife had talked him out of it! I'd imagine that this was a strange conversation for Okolovich.

---

1. Häyhä shot them.

Assassination!

KHOKHLOV: I was sent here to assassinate you, but my wife thinks it's a bad idea.

OKOLOVICH: Please thank your wife for me. Can you come back later? Wait—don't come back later!

KHOKHLOV: Don't worry. I have a conscience, and I'm not going to do it.

OKOLOVICH: Well, *that's* nice to hear. Would you like a crumpet?

Okolovich invited Khokhlov inside, and the two men tried to figure out what to do about the strange situation in which they found themselves. As a result of their meeting, Nikolai Khokhlov defected to the West. He gave press conferences and wrote a book (*In the Name of Conscience*) about his training as an assassin.

But three years later, Khokhlov himself fell mysteriously ill. It turned out that the former assassin was himself the victim of an assassination attempt! The Russian had been poisoned by a radioactive substance that someone put in his coffee.

After getting massive blood transfusions, Khokhlov survived. He moved to California and taught at a university. The assassin with a heart ended up living well into the twenty-first century.

KEEPING SECRETS SECRET!

Nearly a million people in the United States alone have top secret clearance. And you should be one of them! When you apply for a job as a spy, agents will run a background check on you. That means they'll be interviewing people who know you. And one of the most important questions your friends and family will be asked is, "Can [your name] keep a secret?"

The sad thing is, if you don't *already* know how to keep a secret, you'll probably never be able to. You can either do it or you can't! Experts believe that starting about age six, kids start to understand the idea of keeping a secret. Children who get it can then become trustworthy. This is why you can never expect a little kid to keep a secret! (This is also why I refuse to hire any spy under the age of six.)

But some people just don't get it. One wannabe agent confidently told me, "I know what a secret is."

"Okay," I said, "what *is* a secret?"

> A SECRET IS SOMETHING YOU ONLY TELL ONE PERSON AT A TIME.

Wrong.

I fired that kid before he even had the job![1] At least he knew that once you *have* a secret, it's tempting to tell somebody. But if you ever want to get a top security clearance, you must *resist* that temptation.

I encourage you to think about the power you have when you keep a secret. It's a power you only get by never repeating rumors or gossip. Seriously! It shows that

---

1. I felt bad, though, so I gave him a different job as my life coach.

you're trustworthy, and that's how you get to the point where people will trust you with *their* secrets.

Oh, and avoid those people who always try to drag gossip out of you. Who needs the aggravation? If somebody really pushes it, go with the standard spy nonanswer: "I can neither confirm nor deny it." It's not a lie and no information is given. That's good!

SECRETS REVEALED!

One of the strangest things in the history of secrets happened in Germany. After World War II, the country was divided into *West* Germany (a free democracy) and *East* Germany (a communist country controlled by Russia). The East German government kept a constant eye on its citizens. Its leaders were worried that the East Germans would either flee to the West or become spies.

But in 1990, the two Germanys were reunited and became a free democracy! That meant there was no need for the old East German spy agency called the Stasi. And then a politician named Vera Wollenberger helped to pass a law that opened Stasi's top secret files to the public.

Wow! Parents learned that their children had spied on them—and vice versa! A famous human rights worker was discovered to be a spy. There was even a man who learned that his depression came from the drugs his own *doctor* prescribed him. (The Stasi had ordered the doctor to do this.)

As for Vera Wollenberger, she was surprised to discover that her own *husband* was a Stasi informant! Downer. (How do you say "divorce" in German?)

ROSKO! EVEN YOU?

Why were there so many spies and informers? Some people were pressured into it. And an expert said that most "people informed for personal gain, out of loyalty, or simply because they wanted to feel like they had some power."

Germany is still recovering from this avalanche of secrets, which is maybe a good lesson. We should be careful about wanting to know secrets—because we

NOW THESE SPIES COULD KEEP A SECRET

A group of 10 Russian spies were arrested in the United States in 2010. These spies had lived in the States for over 10 years, and nobody aside from FBI agents suspected them of wrongdoing.

One of the suspects went by the name Cynthia Murphy, and she was known as a master gardener. After the FBI arrested the spies, one of Mrs. Murphy's neighbors said, "They couldn't have been spies. [I mean] look what she did with the hydrangeas."

Now that's a good spy![2]

might not like what we discover! (Even so, I still think I'd like to see the FBI files on my family. You see, I have a sneaking suspicion about my brother . . .)

BUT WHO GETS TO KNOW WHAT?

The next time you play miniature golf or enter the octagon for a mixed martial arts match, think of your opponent as the government. And pretend that you're

---

2. The Russians weren't *all* that good, though. One of them once had to write down a false address. So the trained professional wrote "99 Fake Street."

KNOW YOUR SPY AGENCIES!

Oddly, the Federal Bureau of Investigation (FBI) doesn't really have any spies. But it is in charge of *catching* foreign spies and American double agents. Since the FBI is in charge of counterintelligence for the United States, its experts know as much (or more!) about spying as any other intelligence agency.

a reporter! This will help motivate you to win, because reporters *love* to uncover secrets. And the government loves to *keep* secrets.

That means they're archenemies!

But should one side always win against the other? I mean, there are some government secrets that citizens *should* know. But it's impossible to share those secrets with citizens while also keeping them from the government's *enemies*. Although there are many arguments over this, here are some things that almost always need to *stay* secret:

★ Codes and ciphers
★ Identity of spies
★ Location and movement of troops
★ Location and movement of satellites and classified weapons

If an important secret *is* going to be outed, the good should outweigh the bad. For instance, in the 1960s, the US government had a secret plan to invade Cuba. Even though the *New York Times* learned about this plan, the newspaper chose *not* to print the story because American lives might be lost if they did.

So the *Times* sat on the secret. And the Cuban invasion was a total disaster! Not only didn't it work, but lots of people died. Furthermore, the invasion was so lame, the United States looked idiotic for a long time afterward.

So it would have been a lot better for everyone if the *Times had* printed the secret story—but how could its writers have known that? When secrets and ethics and journalism come together, it can be hard to decide on the best course of action.

HE REALLY DISLIKED REPORTERS

A recent US president was well known for calling journalism he didn't like fake news. And other American leaders have also had their issues with reporters. During the Civil War, General William Sherman even tried to have a newsman shot for spying on his troops. (The writer was actually just working on a story.) And upon hearing that three reporters had been killed by artillery, Sherman said, "Good, now we shall have news from hell before breakfast."

Interestingly, there are times when a secret is so important, it's the *spies* who leak them to a news organization. And if a *spy* thinks people should know something, I guess they probably should!

Finally, here's a secret about secrets: after a while, they lose all their power. Think about it. What was your most embarrassing secret when you were five? Perhaps you got caught picking your nose in class. Or maybe you wet your bed at a sleepover. Who cares! (Please ignore these examples if you are six.)

The point is, the all-important secrets that spies die for today are often just *interesting* secrets in a few short years.

And that's why I can't think of *any* secret that should be kept secret forever. Even the fact that I love cupcakes with pink frosting. (Hey, don't laugh. You picked your nose in kindergarten!)

THE BEST (AND WORST!) SECRET NAMES EVER!

"The Great Game."

That's the name that British agents once used for spy work. And espionage *is* just like a game. You know like how in Monopoly when you get interrogated if you can't explain exactly *why* you have an extra $200 after passing Go? (That's how we play at my house, anyway.)

Once you get your top secret clearance, you'll be joining a group of other intelligence agents. So what cool code name should you call yourselves? There are different approaches you could take. For instance, the CIA is sometimes called "The Company" or "The Firm." *Bor-ring.* And there's a private spy agency called The Analysis Corporation. That's even more of a snoozer!

But I've discovered that these names are lame on purpose. The idea is that if an agency's name is generic enough, people won't notice that these places even exist. So spies are always on the lookout for the most boring ways to describe their offices and agencies.

My research shows that the most boring phrases in the English language are "country music," "math homework," and "basket expert." So the CIA should change its name to something like the CMBE: "Country Music Basket Experts." Once it does this, the spy agency will become magically invisible!

So spies like boring names. Why else would we call ourselves "assets"? We do, as in "we have an asset in their government." (So if you ever hit an agent with your foot, you've kicked his asset!) But if you want to keep things *really* secret, give your spy group an *insulting* code name. For example, what if you called your agency "The Idiots"? Nobody would want to join—in fact, people would avoid you.

SUSPICIOUS PERSON: Hey, what are you guys talking about?
YOU: It's just a meeting of The Idiots. Do you want to be an Idiot?
SUSPICIOUS PERSON (backing away): No thanks! I'll see you Idiots later.

Another good example of this is the Bigot List. In World War II, people in the Allied Command who had access to high-level secrets were on the Bigot List. And naturally, no one else wanted to be added to the Bigot List, so they kept their distance.

On the other hand, you might want *more* members in your secret group. If so, give it the coolest name possible! That's what the founders of the Black Dragon Society did. This Japanese group was formed in 1901. And its leader was named the Darkside Emperor. Ooh, let me sign up! Wait, it was abolished in 1945? Rats.

And then there was the Chinese group from the late 1800s known as the Society of Harmonious Fists (a.k.a. the Boxers). Good one!

Here's one of the longest names I've seen: Extra-ordinary Commission for the Struggle Against Counter-revolution, Espionage, Speculation, and Sabotage. The Russians chose that name for their secret police agency in 1917.

They called it Cheka for short.

One of the most sinister group names in the first half of the twentieth century was the Japanese agency known as the Thought Police. It was charged with making sure that people didn't think bad thoughts. (You don't want to know how they went about figuring this out.)

And one of the best job titles ever came from an Allied unit during World War II. Called the London Controlling Station, the agency's job was to trick German military leaders. So the head of the LCS was called the controller of deception.

Did you see that? The controller of deception! That title is so incredible, I just had to sit down. And after I did, I was inspired to research other interesting code names and spy names from spying history. Like these:

★ Any specialist in the US military is called a "puke." So intelligence agents are known as "intel pukes."

★ Morris Cohen, an agent who worked in China, was known as "Two-Gun." Can you guess why? Oh, I'll just tell you. It was because he always carried *two* guns.

★ During the Cold War, spymaster Markus Wolf (1923–2006) managed 4,000 agents for the East German agency known as Stasi. Wolf was considered the greatest spymaster in the world. He was able to place an agent as a top aide to West Germany's chancellor. (This is like someone planting an agent as vice president of the United States.) For over 20 years, nobody in the West was even sure what he looked like, so Wolf was known as "The Man Without a Face."

★ During World War II, the Japanese had a spy in New York nicknamed "Doll Woman." She was Velvalee Dickinson, the owner of a doll shop. (This was a great cover, BTW.)

★ The Nazis were big fans of opera singer Margery Booth. But what the Nazis didn't know was that Booth helped British prisoners smuggle information by hiding it in her knickers (that is, her underpants). In fact, Booth once performed for Adolf Hitler with secret intelligence in her underwear. Her nickname: the Knicker Spy!

★ Legendary Israeli agent Rafael Eitan was once

IT'S A NOIR, NOIR WORLD

The French word *noir* (nwahr) means black or dark. It's so cool, when the dreaded French spymaster Cardinal Richelieu (1585–1642) created his dastardly intelligence cabinet, he called it the *Cabinet Noir* ("Black Cabinet"). Over time, *noir* has become an excellent word to use for all things dark and sinister!

THE BLACK CABINET

★ *bête noire* (bate nwahr): A person or thing that one particularly dislikes (for example, "Spies wearing spandex body suits are my bête noire").

★ *film noir*: A movie with a strong, dark mood (like *Blade Runner*).

★ *cartoon noir*: A cartoon with a strong, dark mood (such as *Captain Underpants*).

The awesomeness of noir has inspired spies through the years. For instance, after World War I, the United States created an intelligence agency called the American Black Chamber. Scary!

involved in an operation where he had to travel through sewers to blow up a radar station. This earned him the nickname "Rafi the Smelly."

★ Russian security head Nikolai Ezhov was known as "The Bloodthirsty Dwarf." (He was five feet tall.)

One of the best operation code names *ever* had to do with fake Allied offensives in World War II. Operation Hambone started in 1944. In it, an actor was hired to play a British commander. The actor went to locations in Africa and Europe, where he pretended to be planning an invasion in southern Europe. (D-Day would actually be launched on the beaches of Normandy on the northwest coast of France.)

Oh, last thing! During World War II, nobody in Japan could even *say* the name of the Japanese Army's spy agency (Tokumu Bu) without being arrested. That means this *has* to have happened:

"Where do you work?"

"I'd rather not say."

"Seriously, you can trust me."

"It's not a good idea."

"Pretty please?"

"Well . . ." *looks around nervously* "I work for Tokumu Bu."

"You're under arrest."

SPY CATCHING AND LIE DETECTING!

There's an old saying: "It takes a thief to catch a thief." And it takes a spy to catch a spy. That's why counterintelligence was developed. Counterintelligence agencies are in charge of hunting enemy spies and double agents.

And when counterintelligence agents spring into action, they have one thing going for them: enemy spies *stink*.

Of course, *everyone* stinks. But we all stink in our own unique way. That's why the East German spy agency

DIPLOMATIC IMMUNITY?

A man named Mohammed al-Madadi once snuck into the bathroom of an airplane to smoke. That's against the law, so the air marshal on the flight confronted al-Madadi about it. Al-Madadi denied smoking but then made a joke about starting a fire with his shoes.

Not funny! There have been terrorists who tried to hide bombs in their shoes. So al-Madadi was arrested. But witnesses noted that al-Madadi didn't seem to care. Why was he so calm? *Diplomatic immunity.* Mohammad al-Madadi knew he probably couldn't get in any real trouble because he was a diplomat.

Diplomatic immunity means that ambassadors in *any country* can commit *any* crime—from smoking on an airplane to even murder—without being charged with the crime! Of course, no diplomat has ever gone around murdering people. If he did, he'd probably be fired from his job. And without diplomatic immunity, the diplomat might have to go to court after all.

How can this work for you? The next time you are stopped for committing sabotage on a tuna casserole, just claim diplomatic immunity. (And if anyone asks to see your credentials, just say you left them at the embassy!)

Stasi kept a "smell jar" for its suspects. This was a big jar filled with the person's personal items. The idea was that they would smell like the suspect. And if the suspect tried to flee the country, a Stasi hound dog could sniff the smell jar and track the person down.

To get items for the smell jar, Stasi agents would break into a person's apartment when they weren't home and steal them. According to Stasi agents, the best smell item to get was dirty laundry . . . especially dirty underwear. (That *really* smells like the person.)

So yes, East German counterintelligence agents stole dirty underwear. (Man, spy work is sure glamorous!)

Luckily, today's spy agencies have improved on this system. For example, DARPA has been developing electronic noses (e-noses) that can identify specific smells coming from specific armpits. Seriously!

After all, CIA agents have enough things to do besides sniffing armpits. For example, they need to make sure their cover story is airtight. The best kind of cover is government cover. This is for CIA agents in other countries who are posing as regular US government employees.

These spies are also known as "legals," and even "gentleman spies." And their government cover gives the spies a superpower called *diplomatic immunity*.

Diplomatic immunity means if an official CIA spy gets caught spying (or any other naughty activity), they cannot be punished. The worst thing that can happen is the spy can be kicked out of the country, or deported. A spy who's deported is referred to as *persona non grata*: "An unwelcome person."

The number of spies that get declared persona non grata varies from year to year. In 1971, Great Britain expelled 105 suspected spies. And in 2017, Russia expelled 755 Americans from the US embassy!

But if a CIA agent is *not* working under a government cover, everything changes. These spies have what's called a "commercial cover." (They are also sometimes called "illegals.") That means the spies are pretending to work for private companies.

If a spy gets caught while under commercial cover, they can be arrested, imprisoned, and even executed.

Other cover varieties include:

DEEP COVER: Agents under deep cover are put in place years before they are needed. Known as sleeper agents, these spies are always the last ones that anyone suspects. Years ago, East Germany planted 20,000 sleeper agents in other countries. Who knows, maybe some are still out there!

SHALLOW COVER: When a trained agent submerges in the three-foot end of the swimming pool, he's surprisingly hard to spot.

UNDER COVER: The spy in the illustration is catching up on her sleep. Do not disturb.

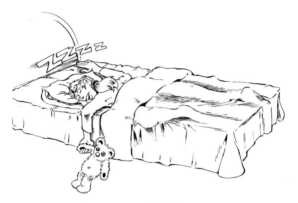

SNAP COVER: A convenient lid for Tupperware.

All these cover choices means that catching a spy is not easy. You have to be tricky!

For instance, when FBI agent Robert Hanssen was suspected of selling American secrets, the first thing his bosses did was *promote* him to a better job.

Were they insane? No. The idea was that promoting Hanssen would make the double agent less suspicious. I mean, why would the FBI promote someone it didn't trust? And this promotion also made it easier for other FBI agents to track his movements.

VOCABULARY

Exfiltration is the opposite of infiltration. It's what a spy does when he tries to sneak *out* of a country.

In Hanssen's case, once the FBI had the needed proof, they arrested him. And it's no picnic for any spy to be *captured* (unless the spy was actually caught *at* a picnic). But while soggy potato salad is bad, SMERSH was worse. That was the name of the spy-catching branch of the old Russian spy agency known as the KGB. Its name came from *Smyert Shpionam,* which means "death to spies." Yikes!

The greatest treasure for a spy agency is catching and interrogating an enemy spy. And as far as I know, the strangest thing a captured spy ever had to keep secret during an interrogation was a poem. That's because British agents who needed to translate top secret codes were once given poems with the code key hidden within them.

Imagine that interview!

INTERROGATOR: We have ways of making you recite poetry.

SPY: I'll *never* reveal my poem to you. Never!

INTERROGATOR (swinging a large wet noodle): Don't make me use this.

SPY: Not the wet noodle! Okay, okay: "The itsy-bitsy spider went up the water spout . . ."

MEAN INTERROGATOR (sitting down): Ooh, I love this one.

THE SCARIEST SPOT IN RUSSIA

The KGB was such a scary spy agency it even inspired its own knock-knock joke:

"Knock knock!"

"Who's there?"

"The KGB."

"The KGB wh—"

"Silence! Nobody questions the KGB!"

KGB headquarters were in a massive Moscow building called Lubyanka, and it doubled as a prison for spies. How bad was Lubyanka? The people who worked there were nicknamed bone crushers. And according to prisoners, Lubyanka was kept as silent as possible. Guards did not speak, but communicated instead by clicking their tongues.

The idea was that all that tongue clicking would be so eerie it would freak out the prisoners. And it did!

For any spy imprisoned in Lubyanka, the greatest hope was to be interrogated and then shipped out to a work camp in Siberia. Although that may not sound so great, it definitely beat the alternatives: torture and death.

And that's why the Russians told this joke:

Q. What's the tallest building in Moscow?

A. Lubyanka. You can see Siberia from its basement!

IF YOU'RE CAUGHT

If you get captured by enemy agents, remember to use a good alibi. That's why you should never start spying without already having a good excuse prepared.

The CIA says any good excuse should be a plausible denial. So you have to deny that you're a spy, and have a believable story to explain yourself. So when a US spy plane (the U-2) was shot down over Russia, the CIA had its plausible denial ready: That wasn't a spy plane, that was an unarmed plane monitoring the weather. So thanks a lot for shooting down our harmless science project, you jerks!

Unfortunately, the captured pilot then confessed to being a spy, which sort of ruined the whole thing.

But it's unlikely that you'll need an excuse as complex as this. Let me think of a possible scenario that you might have to deal with. Got it!

ACCUSATION: You were picking your nose.

PLAUSIBLE DENIAL: A bug flew up your nose, and you were trying to save its life.

Here's the thing—as a spy, you're committing crimes with a secret identity, and your employer doesn't want to admit that you exist. In Russia, they once had a special execution for captured enemy spies called *vyshaya*

187

mera.[1] But luckily, today, many nations are nicer to captured agents. This is partly because death or torture doesn't get anyone good information. Think about it: if someone were threatening you with a hedge trimmer, you'd say *anything* to keep it away from you!

But there are *other* mean things that interrogators might try on you, including:

★ Sleep deprivation
★ Loud noises
★ Bright lights
★ Bribes
★ Brainwashing
★ Hypnosis
★ Annoying music!

Yes, interrogators have been known to play the theme song from *Sesame Street* over and over and over again to wear down a captured spy. (Seriously.)

But if *you* capture a spy, you won't need those interrogation techniques. After all, you have *this* book. Simply read aloud from it to the captured spy. *That* will get results!

---

1. The spy was shot in the back of the head with a huge gun. This makes identifying the person by his face impossible.

THE INTERROGATION: SPOTTING A SPY-ER WHO'S A LIAR

It's easy to tell the truth. That's one reason why most people tell the truth most of the time. It's the *comfortable* thing to do! So during an interrogation, these are signs that a suspect is probably telling the truth:

1. Answers questions completely and directly.
2. Acts attentive and interested.
3. Answers quickly.
4. Gives consistent answers that don't conflict with each other or require explanations.

Ah, but when a person lies, everything changes! Now our suspect has to keep *two* things in mind: the *lie* and the *truth*. This creates conflict, and it makes a person *uncomfortable*. And if someone is uncomfortable, you can spot it.

Before you start your interview, get a clipboard, some paper, and a pen. As your interview starts, watch for any of the following signs. Every time you observe one, mark a little dot on your clipboard. It's easy!

If you have your questions written out beforehand, mark the dots next to the question being asked. This helps locate topics where lies happen. And if this seems like a lot of stuff to look out for, have someone *else* ask the questions. Then you can just keep track of the dots!

Spy Catching and Lie Detecting!

BODY POSITION: Whether seated or standing, everyone has an anchor point. This is a spot where the body weight rests. And a liar may shift anchor points a lot! If seated, he may lean on one elbow and then shift to another one, or bounce his legs. Standing? He may keep switching his weight from foot to foot.

BODY LANGUAGE: Is the person adjusting their glasses, touching their hair, or picking at their fingernails? Are they putting the items around them (like pens or notebooks) in neat little rows? A liar might have lots of body language. So look for touching, rubbing, or tugging on the ears, nose, and eyes, as well as re-adjusting of clothes.

EYES: It's possible to lie with normal eye contact, and research shows liars might even look their questioners in the eyes *more* than usual. But liars may blink more than normal.

VOICE: It is stressful to lie, so a liar's voice tends to go higher than normal. Liars also tend to talk fast. However, if the liar has to invent a lie on the spot, she will slow way down and look upwards as she searches for the best story. If the person is really feeling the stress, there may be stuttering and a lot of pauses and mumbling. Liars also use filler words like *er, um, duh, uh,* or "*help me, I'm a big fat liar.*"

FAKE SMILES AND LAUGHING: It isn't *that* hard to spot a fake smile, because liars only smile with their mouth. A true smile affects the whole face, so that the corners of the eyes will crinkle up. So a thin-lipped, clenched-teeth smile that doesn't crinkle the eyes, might be fake. And a laugh is only real if the person closes his eyes as he laughs. If your suspect starts laughing but is watching you with open eyes, it's as fake as a three-dollar bill.

WORD USE: A liar will often repeat your question back to you. And he might overuse phrases like "To tell the truth," "Really," "Honestly," "Actually," "No kidding," and "Seriously." Also listen for:

★ "Frankly . . ."
★ "To the best of my knowledge . . ."

- ★ "Trust me."
- ★ "Why would I lie?"
- ★ "I swear."
- ★ "You can ask anyone!"
- ★ "... as I said before ..."
- ★ "How dare you ask me that!" or "I can't believe you're asking me that question."
- ★ "How long is this going to take?"

A person who ends statements with "All right?" or "Don't you agree?" or other questions that try to get you to agree to what it was she said is also possibly lying.

Also, a person who is lying uses fewer contractions and emphasizes denials. For example, instead of saying "I didn't do it," she will say "I did *not* do it."

THE QUESTIONS!

You might begin by asking your suspect a nonthreatening question, like "What was the first day at school like?" There's no reason to lie, so pay attention to the way this person tells the *truth*.

As you shift to your real questions, think: Is the person providing the same number of details that he did before? And the way you phrase your questions is also important.

Don't ask specific, confrontational questions like, "When did you become evil?"

Instead, try indirect *leading* questions. These might lead the person to actually talk about the subject. For example, "Why do you think you're in this situation?"

The key is to get your suspect to *talk*. The more a person talks, the more likely he is to feel like getting that secret off his chest. And if you had your suspect tell a story, try this: after the suspect finishes, have him describe everything that happened in reverse! A liar is going to have a *very* hard time doing this, but an honest person can. In fact, while telling the story backwards, the story may gain relevant details!

When you're done, there will rarely be times when you can be 100 percent sure that someone is guilty. After all, an innocent person can fidget. (I'm doing it now!) So look over your dots and see if you spot any patterns on particular questions.

TELLING THE TRUTH: ONCE YOU CAN FAKE THAT, YOU'VE GOT IT MADE

Remember, all of these techniques can also be used on *you*. But while intelligence experts often give classes on how to detect lies, they almost *never* give classes on how to lie. That's because it just doesn't work. Lie detectors are the worst liars around!

But I can give you a few tips:

TRY ANSWERING QUESTIONS WITH QUESTIONS: "Before I tell you about my mission, what's your favorite color?"

CLAIM IGNORANCE: "Wow, how weird that I forgot my own name!"

GIVE OUTRAGEOUSLY GENERAL ANSWERS: "My favorite color? Rainbow."

CHANGE THE TOPIC: "I guess I'm sitting here today because I like pickles. In fact, canning pickles is one of my favorite hobbies. I am especially interested in sweet pickles . . ." and so forth.

AVOID YOUR MOTHER TONGUE!

Chinese spy Larry Wu-Tai Chin took—and passed—lie detector tests even though he was lying. But Chin took these tests in English, and he said he passed the lie detector because it's easier to lie in a foreign language.

NOW WHAT?

After a spy is caught and interrogated, what do you do with them? In the old days, a captured spy might be "terminated with extreme prejudice." But today, we know it's wrong to be prejudiced, so we just kill them.

Ha! Just kidding. Maybe your best option is to try to flip the captured spy. That means you get them to switch over to *your* side and become a double agent. Try to take a positive approach. Like my granny always said, "You catch more spies with honey than with vinegar."

EVE: THE ORIGINAL DOUBLE AGENT?

You've heard the story of Adam and Eve. No espionage there, right? Wrong! The serpent that gets Eve to bite the apple is actually an enemy agent working under the cover of a reptile. This scaly agent flips Eve to his side when he gets her to eat the fruit of knowledge. And then Eve gets Adam to do the same thing. So that means that Eve was tricked into becoming an agent for the other side without even realizing it.

Since most spies get paid for their work, one way to flip a captured spy is to offer her more money than her employer pays. But if you're cheap, you could try simple blackmail. However, many agents (like me!) are so nice, blackmail just won't work!

THE TEN TYPES OF SPY SCREW-UPS!

As you know, spies are very important people. After all, they can help win wars that would have been lost without them. But spies can also *lose* battles that should have been won!

But remember, an epic spy failure for one side is an epic *win* for somebody else. So maybe I shouldn't make such a big deal about it. It's only normal for people to make mistakes. Even me!

Recently, I was assigned to follow a foreign agent. This spy was using an ice cream truck as a cover for his operation. So I reviewed and memorized the information we had on this ice cream mastermind.

Then I imagined myself following the agent without him noticing me. (We spies call this positive visualization, or pretending.) Finally, I had some tea and crumpets before going out on the job. But by the time I got to where my target was supposed to be, he was long gone. Rats!

As I sit here wondering where that ice cream truck is, I'm also thinking about the many kinds of mistakes that spies make. Here are some now!

1. AN ENEMY SPY IS SPOTTED!

In 1970, a CIA agent in Vietnam heard about an enemy spy. This spy was a woman who was selling secret US military documents right on the streets in Saigon.

The CIA agent searched for her, and found the woman disguised as a cookie seller on a street corner. Approaching her, the agent was surprised to find that the enemy agent was selling cookies wrapped in US Navy documents stamped Confidential. Ah-*ha*!

This was obviously a *major* spy ring. In the ensuing investigation, the cookie lady was code-named "Cookie Lady." (How brilliant was that?) CIA agents discovered that the Cookie Lady's papers were coming from the US Naval Office in Saigon. It turned out that a woman who worked at the office was *keeping* the confidential papers she was supposed to burn. Then the office worker was giving the papers to the Cookie Lady for her to wrap her cookies in. But *neither* of the women could read English!

So it turned out that the Cookie Lady was just a cookie lady. (I guess you could say the whole conspiracy was half baked.)

MORAL: That's the way the cookie theory crumbles.

THREATENING BODY ODORS

In 1991, a CIA worker was called down to the agency's parking garage in Virginia. Bomb-sniffing dogs had picked up the scent of something dangerous in his car's trunk! As an armed squad stood by, the employee carefully opened his trunk and revealed the source of the dog's concern: his dirty workout clothes.

2. AN ENEMY SPY IS *NOT* SPOTTED!

Baron August Schluga (1841–1917) was a German spy with mad skills. He was so good, Schluga pulled off tricks that his own side didn't understand. I mean, Schluga's own spymaster didn't even know where the spy *lived*.

In 1914, Schluga (code named "Agent 17") did something extraordinary. At the age of 73, Schluga somehow got his hands on France's entire military strategy! And it was *real*.

This was especially handy since France and Germany were about to go to war. Many experts believe this is the single most amazing feat any spy has ever accomplished. So how did Agent 17 do it? Good question! But Schluga kept his sources and methods secret to the day he died.

MORAL: It's a secret.

KNOW YOUR SPY AGENCIES!

Formed in 1909, MI6 is the United Kingdom's international spy agency. It's like the British CIA. The most famous fictional MI6 employee is Bond ... James Bond. (The "MI" stands for "Military Intelligence," BTW.) The UK also has MI5, which is like the FBI.

3. A FLYING DOUBLE AGENT ISN'T SPOTTED.

When Syria got new Russian fighter jets in 1966, its leaders were excited. These planes were *way* better than anything that Syria's archenemy, Israel, had!

But when a Syrian pilot then flew one of the new fighters to Israel and landed the plane there, it sort of took the fun out of the victory. And when it turned out that Israeli agents had persuaded the pilot to move to Israel, it was all very disappointing.

MORAL: Trust nobody. Suspect everybody!

4. A SPY ISN'T SPOTTED UNTIL WAY TOO LATE.

Larry Wu-Tai Chin joined the CIA in 1952. He was prized for his ability to translate Chinese documents. Good catch! But Larry then sold US secrets to the Chinese government for the next 40 years. He was a mole! This is the word used for spies who hide out in an organization.

MORAL: Don't hire moles. (They're really bad for your lawn.)

5. A SPY SELLS HIS CAMERA ON eBAY?

Some years ago, a man bought a new digital camera on eBay. After taking some photos with the camera, he uploaded them to his computer. But what's this? The camera's memory card already *had* a bunch of photos on it!

These pictures were of missiles, mean-looking bearded men holding rockets, and the fingerprints of the mean-looking men who'd been holding the rockets.

Oh, and there was also information about the encryption codes that the MI6 uses for its computers.

It turned out that an MI6 officer on a terrorist detail had taken the photos. Then he forgot to wipe the memory card clean before selling the camera online.

MORAL: Cover your butt. And wipe the memory card.

6. A SPY SPENDS FIVE CENTS.

In 1953, a Russian spy named Reino Häyhänen spent a nickel in New York City. So what? Well, the spy accidentally used his secret hollow nickel! And this particular hollow nickel contained a coded espionage message on microfilm.

What's Russian for "oopsie"?

The nickel changed hands a few times, and then someone bought a newspaper with it. After the coin came apart, the surprised newsboy could see that it was a fake. Awesome! He turned the fake nickel over to the FBI. The following investigation became known as the Hollow Nickel Case. It took four years and resulted in the smashing of a Russian spy ring and the arrest of an art dealer who turned out to be master Russian spy Rudolf Ivanovich Abel!

And all because someone spent the wrong nickel.

MORAL: Carry exact change.

7. A CLEVER TRICK IS PLAYED!

EXAMPLE A: During World War II, Spain sided with Germany. So when a youth leader from Spain came to England in 1940 to learn about the Boy Scouts, it was a little suspicious. (This youth leader really was a spy.)

The Brits were very kind to the Spaniard and even took him on a flight to Scotland. During this flight, the airplane was passed by endless squadrons of British fighters. The Spaniard was amazed at the hundreds of warplanes he saw! So when the Spanish spy made his secret report back to the Germans, he related that the British air force was *very* powerful. Clearly, invading Great Britain at that time was a *bad* idea.

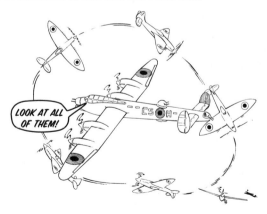

LOOK AT ALL OF THEM!

The only problem was that the British military was actually quite *weak*. The spy had only seen *one* squadron of British fighters . . . it just kept circling around and passing his plane over and over and over!

EXAMPLE B: During World War I, Turkey fought the British in the Middle East. The Turkish forces had an excellent fortress in the town of Gaza. And when one of the Turkish fort's patrols chanced upon a British soldier, its soldiers fired at him. The frightened Brit dropped his backpack, and ran off in a panic.

Inside the blood-soaked backpack, the Turks found British attack plans and a codebook. Score! Using these, they found that the British were planning an attack on Gaza.

The Turks in Gaza got ready for the assault. So they were totally surprised when the British attacked a *different* Turkish stronghold named Beersheba instead. And in the following panic among the Turkish forces, the British took Beersheba, Jerusalem, *and* Gaza.

It turned out that the whole thing had been a setup by the British. And the blood on the pack? It had been smeared on it before the Brit even went out on his patrol.

MORAL: British agents are clever.

8. A SPY HAS *REALLY* IMPORTANT INFORMATION— BUT NOBODY LISTENS!

Dušan Popov (1912–1981) was a true superspy. He was a wealthy playboy and ladies' man who also worked under-cover as a successful secret agent for Great Britain. Popov spoke several languages fluently and even developed his own recipe for invisible ink. Popov was so impressive, writer Ian Fleming partly based James Bond on him.

In 1941, Popov learned of a secret Japanese plan to bomb almost the entire US naval fleet at Pearl Harbor. So he traveled to Washington, D.C., to warn the Americans! A meeting was arranged between Popov and J. Edgar Hoover, the head of the FBI.

With a reputation like Popov's, you'd *think* that Hoover would have paid attention to the agent's warning. No dice. You see, there was one *little* problem with Popov that made Hoover suspicious.

Popov's secret spy code name was "Tricycle"! And the director of the FBI couldn't imagine *why* a spy would have such an odd nickname. It was outrageous! Ludicrous! Suspicious!

So Popov was ignored, and Pearl Harbor caught almost everyone by complete surprise. Everyone except J. Edgar Hoover.

MORAL: Being a little paranoid is healthy. But being small minded doesn't get you anywhere.

9. A SPY IS CAUGHT AND ... HEY, WHERE'D HE GO?

George Blake was a high-level British intelligence agent. He was also spying for Russia from 1953 to 1961.

When Blake was caught, it was believed he had betrayed between 40 and 400 agents. That jerk! Blake was sentenced to prison, but he managed to pull out a loose bar from his jail cell window. Then he climbed down a rope ladder he had knitted himself, and escaped.

Blake escaped from England and traveled to Russia, where he conducted advanced classes for spies.

MORAL: Never let a captured spy knit. (You don't need a sweater that badly.)

10. A GREAT VICTORY TURNS INTO A DASHING DEFEAT!

During World War II, the British ambassador to Turkey left the top secret plans for the invasion of Europe in his personal safe. Bad idea! A spy named Ilyas Bazna, who was working for the Germans, made wax impressions of the ambassador's keys. With the copies he made, Bazna opened the ambassador's safe and photographed papers that gave away a number of Allied secrets, including the *real* plans to D-Day.

Bazna sold his fantastic intelligence to the German military for the equivalent of over a million dollars. And the Germans thought it was worth it! No one could believe how fantastic this information was.

No, seriously, the info was so good, the Germans eventually decided Bazna's information was fake and they never acted on it. (How do you say "Rats" in German?)

As for Bazna, he escaped to Argentina with huge piles of cash. But when the time came to count his earnings, the spy had made a shocking discovery: the money the Germans had paid him was *fake*.

MORAL: You can sometimes trust a spy. But you can *never* trust a Nazi.

Hang on—I think I hear an ice cream truck. Gotta go!

GOING PRO!

So what are the steps to becoming a real spy? Here are some things that couldn't hurt:

PLAY A LOT OF THE BOARD GAME STRATEGO. It's pretty fun, especially when you use the Spy piece to assassinate your opponent's leader.

AVOID GROWING TOO MUCH. The MI5 once listed the perfect height for a male spy as 5 feet, 8 inches. Any taller and the agent might stick out. Any shorter and the agent wouldn't be able to see over a crowd!

DON'T POST DUMB MATERIAL ONLINE. This includes mean YouTube comments and posting photos on Facebook of you bungee jumping without a bungee cord. When people check up on you, the *less* online information they can find, the better.

Of course, even big-shot spies make these kinds of mistakes. In 2009, John Sawers was getting ready to become head of Britain's MI6 (a.k.a. the Secret Intelligence Service). Then his wife posted items about their family on her Facebook page—things like where they lived and worked, who their friends were, and where the family went on vacation. *and* she even posted a picture of Sawers wearing a Speedo. Talk about blowing someone's cover!

BONUS "OOPS!" The MI6 is also in charge of Great Britain's cybersecurity.

WORK ON BEING AMBIDEXTROUS. Think of how impressed the other spy wannabes will be when they find out you can shoot poison darts equally well with either hand! (Plus, if one hand gets injured, you're still dangerous.)

GET GOOD GRADES. Do you know how many spies didn't go to college? Me neither, but I don't think there are very many. And while you're in college, take at least a few international studies courses.

LEARN A FOREIGN LANGUAGE (OR THREE). No pressure, but Sir Richard Burton (1821–1890) was one of the most brilliant spies ever. Part of his success came from the fact that he learned 35 languages.

STAY OUT OF TROUBLE. If you have a gambling problem or a criminal background, you probably won't be hired. My best advice is to hang out exclusively with other people who have read this book.

As a future agent, you should also know the different categories of secrecy. American agencies break it down this way:

CONFIDENTIAL: Whatever you're looking at is kind of, sort of, secret.

SECRET: Anything labeled "secret" is *definitely* secret.

TOP SECRET: This is so secret, it couldn't be any *more* secret!

COSMIC: I lied. Things *can* be more secret! Cosmic secrets are the tip-top secret level of secrecy used by NATO (an alliance of countries including the United States).

Other countries have their own classifications of secrecy. British material could once be classified "most secret." And as if that wasn't good enough, the most sensitive level was "hush most secret."

I hope you agree with me that it's not very impressive when spies use the word *hush*. And there's another category for secrets that can only be whispered:

EARS ONLY: This must be the most secret of them all! The category of "ears only" is given to any information that is so *totally* outrageously secret, it must not be written down. Ears only has to be said, and then, only in supersafe areas that have been debugged.

YOUR APPLICATION

Okay, so now you're ready to apply to an intelligence agency. Good luck! Your hiring process will go like this:

1. PAPERWORK. You'll have to turn in *lots* of forms. The spy agency will especially want to know if you're an honest person who is loyal to your country. In addition to the usual questions about your past, they'll *really* want to know if you've ever gotten in trouble for hacking. (And hopefully, you haven't . . . or if you have, you're so good that it's a plus.)

2. TAKING PSYCHOLOGICAL TESTS. The agency wants to know if you are a stable, organized person. You will also be scored in personality categories like:

   ★ Are you outgoing? A show-off? Really shy? Insane?

   ★ Are you open to new experiences? Are you closed to old experiences? Insane?

   ★ Are you a trusting and agreeable person? Paranoid? Gullible? Insane?

3. TAKING LIE DETECTOR TESTS. Obviously, the idea is to

find out how honest you are. But just as important is how you deal with pressure. One of the favorite tricks that polygraph questioners love to play is this: during the exam, the questioner will say, "And now, this is the *most important question* on the exam."

4. THE BACKGROUND INVESTIGATION. This is where your friends, relatives, former coworkers, and fellow students will get asked things like:

★ Does she have any issues?

★ Would you consider her trustworthy?

★ Does she know any foreigners? Who? How often does she see them?

★ Has she read any books by Bart King? She has?

Don't you love that guy? You *don't*?! Are you insane?

YOU'RE HIRED! (NOW YOU'RE A MORON.)

Let's say you got the job. Congratulations! Now you get to start learning some *secrets*. But being a spy with top secret clearance has its dangers! When an intelligence expert named Daniel Ellsberg received his top security clearance, another agent warned him about the stages he would go through:

1. You're excited by all of the top secret things you're learning. Being a spy *rules*!
2. You feel like a fool for the times you criticized leaders like the president. They had top secret info and you *didn't* . . . and you thought you knew better?
3. After about two weeks, you think anyone who doesn't have a top secret clearance like yours is an idiot. After two more years of this, you can't learn from anybody who doesn't have top secret clearance. That's because you're always thinking, "She doesn't know what I know." So no matter how smart the experts are, you ignore them!

4. You are now a moron.

Of course, if you know you might become a moron, you can prevent it from happening! And another good way to avoid becoming a moron is to travel to secret spots where you can study intelligence with the best spies out there.

One place you might be able to get into is Disneyland's supersecret Club 33. It's in the New Orleans Square part of Disneyland, and there are others in Disney World. Just go to the Blue Bayou Restaurant and look for the 33 Royal Street address. You'll only see a door there—but if you're a club member, that door will open! Normal people have to pay as much as $100,000 to join; the annual membership fee can be $30,000. And recently there was a 14-year waiting list! But with your security clearance, you should be able to go in and enjoy Club 33's amazing [description deleted by Disney security].